To Mike,
God's Blessings to

Jeff Goldberg

MW00887400

BLIND AUTHORITY

by Jeffrey M. Goldberg

Dedication

To Mom, whose love and passion for her family endures.

To my wife, children and their spouses, who are
simply the best people I know.

To all people who face adversity and in need of encouragement.

Acknowledgements:

I could not have written this book without the skillful eyes and hands of my editor, Stephen Bauer. Steve and I (and our wives) forged a friendship while as a newspaperman he wrote about the misfortunes of the bible cult I was involved with. I received excellent feedback on the final rough draft from my wife, daughter Leah, my mother and good friend, Ron Strack. Jeff Goldberg – August 6, 2011.

CONTENTS

Author's Note xi

Introduction xv

I. JEWISH ROOTS, MICHIGAN CHILDHOOD 19

II. SECULAR YOUTH, SPORTS SUCCESS 31

III. INFORMED DECISION 43

IV. RIVER OF SEPARATION 58

V. INTERVENTION 75

VI. THE FELLOWSHIP CHANGES 92

VII. EXPECT THE UNEXPECTED 109

VIII. BORN AGAIN, AGAIN 119

Afterword 134

Author's note:

My hope in writing the story is that others can see something for their own personal growth and well-being. Throughout my life I have been encouraged by others; my parents, siblings, friends and even people I don't know. Mostly, I feel comfort reading the bible and the promises of God. Although a topic of great debate throughout the Ages, I believe His Word is perfect. I have made mistakes in judgment and take full responsibility for my actions but I know, as it states in both the books of Joshua and Hebrews, God will never leave me or forsake me.

I was part of a group that evolved into a bible cult for nine years, but left it in August of 1983. Enough time has elapsed to allow me to see clearly what I went through and what my family experienced. This sect evolved from a bible study group of sincere, faithful believers into behaviors that included shunning families, vandalizing other churches and controlling lives of its members.

Cult members turned away from their own families, thinking their religion required it and that the group was their "real family".

Martha Keller, mother of Doug and Denny Keller, who were key leaders in the fellowship, said in an interview in 1986, that she had been shunned by her sons.

"You can't be a Christian and cut off your parents," Mrs. Keller said. "You can't be a Christian and cut off your grandparents and deny them their grandchildren. They call themselves Christians. They are not. They are causing a lot of pain, a lot of hurt to parents and grandparents."

Martha Keller's brother said of his nephews, "I think they are acting as God rather than preaching the Word of God."

Families thus shunned were stunned, asking themselves, "Where did we go wrong?" Often, the answer was that they had done nothing unusual, nothing wrong; their loved ones felt something that they had not felt before. Too often, the answer was the leaders of this change were proud of the changes they made; too often, they looked to themselves for the answers and, too often, that was the problem.

Early on, after leaving the cult, I felt somewhat embarrassed about having been in a cult and it was difficult talking about it among friends, let alone publicly. Now that I feel more comfortable, I think it is important for people to hear my story, my testimony, of how a Jewish man comes to know the Messiah and the ensuing consequences. There are evangelical Christians who, after reading this story, may want to have an intelligent dialogue with God's Chosen People. This book describes my journey to salvation and forgiveness of sins.

Unfortunately, there are many cults out there. They will always be with us and perhaps I can shed some light on how to deal with them. Periodically, there is headline news about some cult that has affected a celebrity, or there are suicides—for example, the 'Heavens Gate' cult was news during the Spring 1997 and the Detroit Militia Group in 2010.

Cults, of course, can be religious or non-religious. Cult leaders control people's lives and minds. There are some consistencies in cults, some objective parameters that you can look at to find out if they are a cult and how to deal with them. Bear in mind, though, this is not a thesis on why a cult leader becomes one. I have no special background regarding any dysfunction in a cult leader's life or possibly strange psyche of cult members that draws a person to this type of evil. I can only report actions and conversations I was a part of or witnessed.

I do not keep a daily journal, however, I have a habit of writing notes and retaining newspaper articles after major life events and therefore able to piece together timelines and facts throughout the various stages of my life. I believe it is very important to be accurate; however, I have changed the names of most people, or simply used first names, to protect them and their families. Everyone I write about has moved on to better and even great things since the dark days of the cult. There is no need to publicly vilify or embarrass anyone here. God's grace has been more than sufficient to me therefore I can show a little grace to others as well.

I hope this book encourages the reader in whatever dilemma they may find themselves. No matter what problems and challenges we face something good can happen. I have learned over the years that God's promises are real because God is real.

"Cease striving and know that I am God; I will be exalted among the nations, I will be exalted in the earth." Book of Psalms chapter 46, verse 10.

INTRODUCTION

If the statistics are right, the Jews constitute but 1 percent of the human race. It suggests a nebulous, dim puff of star dust in the malaise of the Milky Way. Properly, the Jew ought hardly to be heard of, but he is heard of, has always been heard of.

He is as prominent on the planet as any other people, and his commercial importance is extravagantly out of proportion to the smallness of his bulk. His contributions to the world's list of great names in literature, science, art, music, finance, medicine, and obtuse learning are also way out of proportion with his members.

He has made a marvelous fight in this world in all the ages, and he has done it with his hands tied behind himself.

He could be vain of himself and be excused for it. The Egyptians, the Babylonians, and the Persians rose, filled the planet with sound and splendor, and faded to dream stuff and passed away. The Greeks and

Romans followed and made a vast noise and they are gone. Other peoples have sprung up and held their torch high for a time. But it burned out, and they sit in twilight now, or have vanished.

The Jew saw them all, and is now what he always was, exhibiting no decadence, no infirmities of age.

Mark Twain – Harper's Magazine, September 1899.

How did a nice Jewish boy from Detroit, a successful athlete with good family ties, get involved in a cult in Illinois? How did he manage to keep his head and heart straight after he was kidnapped twice?

B y December 1977, I had gone from star high school athlete in the Detroit suburbs to college football at the University of Illinois; from Jewish boy to born-again Christian Jewish believer in a fundamental evangelical group; from hoping to marry my hometown high school sweetheart to engagement to a Christian girl on a university campus. That was all quite a shock to my family.

So, they had me kidnapped by professionals who attempted a deprogramming; to rescue my mind from a cult, not just once, but twice.

The first time, two days before Christmas that year, I was on my way to the University of Illinois campus in Urbana, Illinois, when two strangers appeared and showed me a court order stating that I had to go with them to Chicago. They told me my mother wanted to see me. They explained that she had been appointed by the court as my temporary guardian.

When I arrived with them in Chicago, my mother and stepfather were waiting. She said, "I love you and we are doing this to help you." I found out later she was concerned about my mental health and spiritual well-being due to sudden changes and actions by me.

After four days in Chicago, the deprogramming moved to Florida. The idea was to be separate from the religious group, to make sure my decisions were my own, particularly my impending marriage. The deprogrammers pushed me to return to my Jewish roots. I told them, as I had before, that it is natural for a Jew to become a follower of Jesus.

On Jan. 5, my fiancée flew down to Florida. By the time she left, four days later, we had a plan: postpone our wedding, I would move back to Michigan to show my parents that all was well, and to finish my college degree.

Ultimately, we returned to the Champaign-Urbana area, finding a place in a new church and building a family of our own. So, our story continues.

I.

JEWISH ROOTS, MICHIGAN CHILDHOOD

W hen I was born in 1955, mom kept a kosher home. My paternal grandparents (who adopted my dad when he was a child) were very religious people following the Jewish Orthodox rites. Grandpa Dave and Grandma Fanny Goldberg attended synagogue often for services and Grandpa even co-founded two synagogues in the Detroit area. Coincidentally, in the early 1950s, he donated money to the campus Hillel Foundation building fund at the University of Illinois, my alma mater.

At a young age, Grandpa Dave migrated to Detroit from Latvia in the early 1900s and married Fanny, who was from Scotland. At Ellis Island his name was changed from Golon to Goldberg.

By the 1930s, he was a very successful businessman, owning East Side Coal Company in Detroit. He was a humble, kind and generous soul with an impeccable reputation in the city of Detroit. When my parents divorced, my dad, Moris Goldberg, was unable to support my mother, Dolores, and her three children. As a result, Mom worked and Grandpa paid the home mortgage. One of our special joys was receiving bags of bagels on our front porch from Grandpa Dave every Sunday.

We lived in a quiet, predominantly Jewish neighborhood in a suburban town called Oak Park.

Mom was a hardworking, single mother who did a great job raising us. She saw to it we had food, clothes, a roof over our head and proper health care. After her divorce, she became manager of a ladies clothing store and later a jewelry store. She eventually took some business courses and became a secretary. Mom has a fantastic singing voice and is a very talented theater person. She has excellent stage presence and I believe she would have been a successful musical theater actress if she hadn't chosen the joys of motherhood. Mom even recorded a song when she was 16 years old. Her mother, Shirley, also a talented songstress, was always asked to sing at weddings, bar mitzvahs and other special occasions. "Nana," as we called her, was a special person who lit up the room when she entered. She was a first-generation American Jew born in Connecticut. Her family surname was Teplitsky, which was later changed to Taylor. She married Grandpa Hy and they owned and managed jewelry stores in the Detroit area.

One of my great grandparents came from Kiev, Ukraine, Russia, in the mid to late 1800s. Due to the pogroms, he decided to desert the army and head for America with his wife posing as his sister.

There is a rumor in our family that one of our immigrant ancestors was a horse thief and left Russia before getting caught. In May 2008, I went on a mission trip to Kiev. The librarians and government officials appreciated my relatives' stories but, they could not find any family links to me directly.

Mom and Moris were married at a young age immediately after high school. My oldest sister, Sheryl, was born May 1949, one month before mom turned 18. My second sister, Ruthellen, was born three years later and I was born three years after that in Detroit, Michigan. I was the first son, which is very important in a Jewish family, not only to sustain the name, but also to carry on the traditions of the Jewish faith.

When my parents divorced, I was five years old and too young to understand what the permanent separation meant. I felt a little lost not seeing my dad around on an every-day basis. It was later explained to me they were geared to go in different directions in their lives and decided to split up. I had thoughts of never marrying so I would never feel that pain again. I didn't understand marriage and love can last a lifetime. During grade school, I saw dad on a monthly basis, but very little in junior and senior high school.

I got along well with my sisters, but like most families, we had our youthful conflicts. When I was about five years old, we were playing a game and they locked me in the front of the house entrance vestibule. I became upset and broke the glass to get out and my arm was bleeding profusely. Mom rushed me to Beaumont Hospital and they sewed me up with 22 stitches on my wrist. That was a close call; I vividly remember the blood soaked towel.

When I was in first grade, we moved to another part of town. I enrolled in a new school and made new friends. There were a lot of Jewish kids my age on the same street. Gary, Steve, and Mark introduced me to organized baseball and flag football in the park district.

During the summer after fourth grade, my friends were playing softball under the WLDM radio tower and as we picked sides my sister, Ruth, was chosen ahead of me. I was very upset a girl, let alone my sister, was better than me. That is when I decided I would become a great athlete. I vowed to never be picked lower than first in any sport. I like to remind my family, Ruth and my grade school friends are indirectly responsible for me playing college football at the University of Illinois.

During my grade school years I attended Yeshiva Beth Yehudah, an orthodox afternoon school for training in the Jewish Torah, prayer and traditions. Although by this time, after the divorce, we didn't keep a strict kosher home, mom made sure I had training to understand the Jewish lifestyle and our history. Rabbi Kahn was my favorite teacher. He was a roundish man with a beard and traditional pais (locks growing from sideburns) who taught from the Torah in an understanding way. He also had a great hook shot on the basketball court that no one could stop.

During the Jewish holiday Passover each year, our families would rotate as to who would serve the enormous meal. My maternal grandparents, uncle, and mom would take turns. We met on the first and last night of Passover. "Uncle" Leo (not my uncle, but my uncle's father-in-law) would lead the Passover Seder service in the Hebrew language and traditions. All the children would sit patiently, waiting during prayers and story telling for 20 or 30 minutes before the meal would be served.

There are several major holidays in the Jewish calendar and Passover (Pesach) is probably the most known throughout the non-Jewish world. It is the story of God's intervention through Moses to free the Hebrew slaves from Egyptian rule. It takes place in early biblical times and there are 10 plagues placed upon the Egyptians.

The final plague, killing of the first born, was avoided by the Hebrews, who followed God's instructions to kill a lamb without blemish and place the blood around the door posts. The family then cooked and ate the lamb. During that awful night, the angel of death, seeing the blood on the doorway passed over the marked homes and, therefore, the first born in each family avoided certain death. The Egyptians could not escape God's wrath that night.

Although a story of death, with reminders of the suffering of the Jews in Egypt, it is also a story of triumph: how the Hebrews, with the mighty hand of God (and the release by Pharaoh), were led out of Egypt by Moses for the land of milk and honey, Israel. The Hebrews left in such haste that they ate unleavened bread (matzo) because there was no time to use yeast and allow the dough to rise. It was not an easy trip. Early in their exodus the Hebrews decided to worship golden idols, drink freely and perform acts of debauchery. For these sins, God waited for a new generation of Hebrews to be born to enter Israel. It took the Hebrew nations forty years, wandering the desert, to reach its Promised Land.

Another Jewish holiday of triumph is Hanukkah. About 400 BCE (before Common Era), the Assyrians took over Jerusalem and desecrated the Temple. A revolt was begun by Judah and the Maccabees who eventually ran the Assyrians out of town. It was this little band of Jewish guerrillas that drove out a powerful army from Jerusalem; a David and Goliath type story. If that wasn't miracle enough, when the temple was restored and rededicated – Hanukkah means 'to dedicate' – there was one cruse of oil for the eternal lamp for one day of light. While helpers went to other cities to find more oil, the lamp stayed lit for a miraculous eight days. Thus, to this day, the holiday of Hanukkah, commemorating another Jewish victory, lasts eight days.

Over the last 100 years or so, Hanukkah evolved into a holiday where, in some homes, along with the traditional lighting of candles each night, there is gift-giving to the children. They play with dreidels (spinning tops) and receive Hanukkah gelt (money). Growing up, my sisters and I always looked forward to Hanukkah and its festivities.

The Jewish synagogue is open every day for prayer and services. However, the time of year when most Jews go to service is during the Ten Days of Awe (late summer). It begins with the Jewish New

Year (Rosh Hashanah) and ends on the Day of Repentance (Yom Kippur). From blowing a ram's horn (shofar), Rosh Hashanah is a happy celebratory event to a highly solemn day of fasting on Yom Kippur, reminding oneself of your sins and asking God to cleanse you from your ugly deeds of the past year. As I reached my teen years, I recall dreading Yom Kippur because I didn't like to fast and became hungry relatively early in the day.

There are other significant holidays our family observed to a lesser degree throughout the year, such as Purim, Shavuos and Sukkos. It has been said that there is a Jewish event that can be celebrated every day. I guess that is what happens when you have a group of people who have been around over 5700 years. A common joke at Jewish feasts is to say, "They tried to kill us. We Won. Let's eat!"

There are three main branches of the Jewish faith: orthodox, reformed and conservative. Orthodox Jews are devoted to strictly following the law as written in the Torah. There are 613 command-ments (mitzvos) in the Torah they live each day to fulfill. You may have seen or read about orthodox men in black suits and hats with beards and pais. They keep the Sabbath by attending the synagogue (shul), not driving a car or doing any work. They observe the kosher dietary laws (e.g. not eating pork or mixing dairy with meat at the same meal). Women are separate from men in the synagogue, and the men wear kippahs or head coverings at all times. Orthodox Jews pray three times a day, everyday.

For the reformed Jews the dietary laws are not observed strictly. Hope for a personal Messiah is replaced with the hope for a messianic time of peace for humanity. The Reform movement began in Germany, but is now centered in the United States. Generally, those who observe Reformed Judaism still believe in the Hebrew bible (Tenach), but also believe in progressive revelation, which takes into account changes that occur throughout history. Reformists attend temple, not synagogue. Genders mix in the services. Mostly English is used and musical instruments are permitted during services. Reformists run the spectrum of believers in God to atheists. Many are Jews merely because they come from a Jewish background, more cultural than religious. They may or may not keep kosher and usually do not attend daily services.

The Conservative Jew sees Jewish culture as the unifying bond for Jews. The largest numbers of affiliated Jews belong to this group. **(Note 1)** My family was conservative in their beliefs and activities. We observed the holidays, but rarely attended shul. I appreciate my Jewish roots, having an understanding of God and enjoyed the fruits of being free to do what I want in America. That is not to say that all was rosy. Some time after I told my sister, Sheryl, I was a believer in Jesus the Jewish Messiah, she told me about verbal exchanges with anti-Semites (Jew-haters). She told me when in high school she was called a "Christ-killer". This is not an uncommon epithet for people to call Jews. Some so-called Christians believe if Jews did not live everyone would be better off. What those people don't seem to understand is that Jesus gave his life freely, not just to fulfill prophesies of death and his resurrection, but also for the benefit of *all* mankind for forgiveness of sin and eternal life with God the Father. The Jewish leaders of the day, along with the Romans, were merely a conduit to accomplish God's forecasted goals for eternal redemption.

Generally, I had no religious problems while in junior and senior high school. The friends and athletes I hung around only cared about girls, sports and schoolwork, probably in that order of importance. Religion was never part of our discussions.

One month before my 10th birthday, mom married Merrill. At first, I rebelled when mom told us about the impending remarriage. At the ripe old age of nine, I had been the man of the house for four years and I had to give that up. But, I got over it. Merrill was a wonderful fellow and a great father. He raised us. He had three children from his first marriage, and my mom had three children from her first marriage and together they had a son. So, we had a very big family. We didn't all live under the same roof, but we got together on Sundays, and always enjoyed each others' company. Each child had a step-sibling in a similar age range. I still get a kick telling people I have a sister who is three months older than me. Most people look at me cock-eyed for a moment or two, and then figure it out before I confirm the truth.

One of my favorite events growing up was when I became a Bar Mitzvah. Bar Mitzvah means "Son of the Law" and it is time when a Jewish boy turns 13 years of age and leads certain portions of service at the synagogue. It marks a point in his life of "becoming a man" and is responsible for following all the rules, regulations, rituals and traditions of the Jewish faith. I thoroughly enjoyed learning to read Hebrew musical notes in the Torah and Siddur (prayer book). I had a slight fascination for the history of the Jewish people. Although I learned about the Orthodox ways, I could not conceive myself following them. Fortunately, mom was more Conservative and Reformed in her views and walk in her Jewish life.

Initially, I encountered some stage fright appearing on the raised platform or stage (bimah) in front of hundreds of people during my Bar Mitzvah service at the synagogue my Grandpa Dave founded. I confidently recited Hebrew prayers and sang passages from two different portions of the Hebrew scrolls: the five books of Moses (Torah) and histories, prophets and poets (Haftora).

After the service, my folks hosted a lavish party for me. There were about 150 relatives and family friends in attendance, as well as about 20 of my friends. It was loads of fun dancing with the girls and receiving all the attention. There were also gifts, mostly cash and stock certificates. I recall receiving stocks for K-MART, which was then headquartered in suburban Detroit. I eventually cashed them in when I got married.

In 1970, Mom and Merrill started their own business. Merrill worked in senior management for a Detroit steel distributor for many years and my parents decided to begin their own steel brokerage operation. After a few years, it became very successful. My parents attained some affluence and donated time and money and hosted fundraising events for various Jewish causes and other research and non-profit organizations. I learned great lessons from my parents, at a young age, that if you have a lot you should give a lot. At the end of my college freshman year I decided to work for Merrill and learn the steel business. I learned many aspects of the operation: prospecting and trying to make sales, about the product: angle iron, channels, beams, flats, coils, sheets, pickled and oiled and so on. My mom's brother was the general manager and handled the shipping of the steel, so I learned how to do that as well. I must say that I was not very successful at sales. I recall my first sale was to a steel fabricating company, somewhere in Pennsylvania, and I may have gotten another sale or two of a truckload of product, but there weren't too many. I was young, 19, at the time, and I really didn't have the sale-savvy or confidence to overcome rejections. It was a difficult, but worthwhile summer, particularly learning how to sell product.

My sisters were, and still are, a very important part of my life. Growing up, I was particularly close to Ruthellen. We had our own secret language and spoke in a kind of frog voice when we were pre-teens. We even communicated with our own type of Morse code in the middle of the night, knocking on the bedroom wall that separated us. Ruth loves animals. She was always bringing a stray dog or cat home and we had several birds. I recall mom washing a bird called Cutie in the kitchen sink with a sprayer and ended up drowning it. It was not a happy moment in our lives. Sheryl dated several guys in high school and between my two sisters I learned many things kids learned in the 1960's to get by.

NOTE 1 – "How to Respond to Judaism", Erwin J. Kolb, Concordia Publishing House, 1990, pp10-11.

II.

SECULAR YOUTH, SPORTS SUCCESS

Athletics was an important part of my youth. Little did I know at the time where that path would lead. I lettered in four different sports in high school and had sports-related surgery twice. I was all-conference in football my junior year and honorable mention all-state in football and track my senior year. I considered myself a true scholar-athlete as I was a member of the National Honor Society.

In my junior year in high school, our football team was in the midst of an undefeated season and one night I experienced a toke of marijuana with a group of friends after a game. First thing Monday morning, the head coach called me into his office and told me if he ever heard again I did any drugs I'd be off the team in a flash. Well, I didn't much care to hurt my body with drugs in the first place and, secondly, I loved playing so it was an easy life decision on my part. What I never found out was how the coach heard about it so quick.

Apparently, word got out to the student body over the weekend that big deal athlete Jeff Goldberg smoked dope.

I'm not sure how, but I tore my medial meniscus cartilage in my left knee and had surgery immediately after the baseball season of my junior year. I recuperated quickly and was ready for my senior year of football in time for double sessions (two a day practices) in August. My second major injury, a dislocated shoulder, occurred during a football game in the middle of the season of my senior year.

Immediately after the injury, my parents wanted me to stop playing, but I wouldn't hear of it. I was familiar with one of the former great Detroit Lions' running back, Mel Farr, who played with a harness on each arm to prevent his shoulder from popping out. I saw the orthopedic doctor who fixed my knee and he set me up with the harness. Before each practice and game, I placed a leather strap around my chest and a smaller strap around my left bicep. A chain running between the two prevented my arm from moving too high over my head when it would usually pop out of place. The crazy contraption worked. I continued the season and played pretty well. I earned all-conference and all-state honors and college recruiters were calling on me. I eventually had surgery during the basketball season. The basketball team didn't miss me much on the court because I was basically the fourth guard in a three-guard offense. The coach didn't run the three-guard offense very often anyway.

I was recruited by the Ivy League, Mid-America Conference (MAC) and most of the mid-major state schools. I recall going on my invited visit to the University of Illinois in February of my senior year with my arm still in a sling from surgery. I thought the injury and surgery would kill my chances of playing in the Big Ten, but Illinois offered me a chance to come to campus as a preferred walk-on and earn a scholarship. I came very close to attending an institution in my home state. Although not recruited to play football, just before my weekend visit at Illinois I turned in my room deposit at Michigan State University.

The University of Illinois has a great College of Business and if football didn't work out I was going to get an excellent education. My parents, knowing how much I loved football, reluctantly approved the plan. They were hoping I'd attend an Ivy League school (University of Pennsylvania and Cornell recruited me) or even the Sorbonne in Paris. Going overseas was not in my plans.

During my high school years, I worked part-time during the summers at different places for minimum wage; usually at a dime store stocking shelves. I was a very good student and loved sports. In high school I earned eight varsity letters in four different sports with great success and publicity. I meticulously kept track of both academic and athletic honors in several scrapbooks along with trophies earned on a shelf in my bedroom. Southfield-Lathrup High School, where I attended, had over 3000 students and had a winning program in several sports. In addition to the football offers I received before deciding on the University of Illinois, I was offered a minor league baseball contract with a major league team. Mom nixed that in a hurry and I was happy to oblige. College first!

I arrived on the University of Illinois campus in early August 1973, reporting to the football team and thrilled to be part of a Big Ten program. While being recruited at Southfield-Lathrup High School, I decided I was either going to play in a Division I school, particularly in the Big Ten, or wasn't going to play college football at all, so, I was very glad to be in Champaign-Urbana. Other athletes were arriving and meeting the coaching staff at the football stadium. According to stories in the local newspapers over the next few days, our recruiting class was counted as one of the best in Illinois since the 1963 Rose Bowl team. We had High School All-Americans from Philadelphia, Chicago, and other large cities. Bob Blackman was the head coach, in the second year of a five-year contract, and had reasonable success his first year, installing new offensive and defensive systems. Before coming to Illinois, Blackman had great success coaching in the Ivy League. He was at Dartmouth College, and won eight league championships before arriving at Illinois.

As the freshmen athletes arrived and checked in, we became reacquainted with the coaching staff. Over the next couple of days, the upperclassmen reported, and we started our daily double sessions. In the evening, we had sessions with our playbooks and coaches in a classroom setting. By the second week, we wore full pads in the morning and in the afternoon. Double sessions were grueling, and in the Central Illinois area of Champaign-Urbana, the start of football season was very hot; well over 80 degrees and very humid.

I reported to camp to play a position called swing-back, which, in the Blackman multiple offense, was a combination of wide-receiver and running back. This was advantageous to me because my high school football team ran a similar multiple offense. I was familiar with the type of system, and it helped me to understand the playbook before reporting to camp. Also, I was not a big guy at 5 feet 10 inches tall, about 160 pounds, so my background helped me compete with the bigger guys. I think this was the first or second year freshmen were eligible to play on varsity, which also helped because a couple players were moved up to varsity. I used the year to my advantage by lifting weights and become faster and stronger and work on my pass-receiving skills that would help me later.

At the time, football teams were allowed to have a varsity reserve schedule, sometimes called a "junior varsity" schedule of three to six games competing against other universities. The only problem with playing on the varsity reserve schedule is that it uses one year of eligibility. In college football, you are allowed to play in games four years over a five-year span. In other words, you have one red-shirt year (a year you can sit out) and not play any competitive games, and save a year of eligibility for when you're older. That's why so many football athletes are in school for four-and-half or five years while non- athletes usually finish in four years. All in all, I felt pretty good about my position on the depth chart for the football team.

I recall early on in double sessions the freshmen were scrimmaging against the varsity. I broke through the line, got a sizeable gain, was tackled and while laying flat on my back a big foot stomped on my chest and the foot stayed there. Standing over me was Ty, varsity captain linebacker, and he said, "If you ever do that again, I'll bust your butt!" or similar words, trying to really throw the scare into me. I got a chuckle out of it and went back to the huddle.

About the eighth or ninth day of double sessions, it got to be grueling, with all the hitting and learning and drills and I started to feel homesick. I was dating a girl at home in suburban Detroit and I was 400 miles away. I missed home cooking, my girlfriend, felt very lonesome and a little depressed. I sat on one of the benches by my locker in the freshmen locker room. As I sat there, nearly in tears, the head freshmen football coach came to me and asked what was going on. He put his arm around my shoulder and we talked a little bit. He made me feel comfortable and at ease. He told me it was a natural thing to go through, to just hang in there and stick it out. Everything will be fine once school gets going and I make a few friends.

I'm sure part of what I was going through was being a little fish in a big pond. In high school I had huge success in several sports at a time when I was a big fish in a little pond. However, the coach was right. I stuck it out through double sessions, became busy with school work and I made some friends that helped with some of the loneliness and ego problems.

My roommate is named Dan Beaver, who, reporting in as a freshman, won a starting job as a place-kicker. Since Dan and I were both late recruits to join the team, we roomed together in the dormitory our freshmen year. Perhaps God planned how we ended up rooming together.

Dan was born in Africa, son of Christian missionaries. By the time he was in high school, he was living in California, near Newport Beach, California. He was about 6'1", 175 pounds, very athletic, and loved the game of basketball. In fact, John Wooden, former UCLA basketball coach, was his favorite coach. Dan and I, when we had free time, went over to the campus recreation building and played basketball.

Dan was a redhead and had a high school sweetheart by the name of Tori, who he later married. Dan has four grown children now, and is a Christian missionary in the Philippines teaching at a school for missionary kids. He has an outreach to young children and coaches basketball.

Dan has a very strong faith in Jesus Christ and rooming with him was my first encounter with somebody who was evangelistic in his belief in Jesus Christ. He was not a very outspoken person and didn't go around sharing the gospel at the drop of a hat. He had a very successful freshmen year on the varsity football team in which he kicked a lot of field goals during the season. In a game against

Purdue, he scored all the points, set a Big Ten school record and tied the national record by kicking five field goals in one game. We won 15-13. When it hit the papers the next day, Dan honored his teammates and gave all the glory to God in a very sincere way. Success of this kind can really go to an athlete's head and give him a big ego, but Dan handled it with humility. I was very impressed by his mature attitude in the midst of all his success.

During the course of the season, we had four or five varsity reserve games, in which I either started or alternated starting with another freshman swing-back. His name is Dave, who hailed from Munster, Indiana, and we became good friends.

Classes went well. Although a national honor society student in high school, I had to work harder for grades in college. I carried a 'B' average for first few semesters in the College of Business majoring in Management Science. On weekends, when the varsity was playing away from home and there would be no varsity reserve games, I drove home to Detroit to see family, friends and my girlfriend.

All in all, my first freshman semester at the University of Illinois was very good, a highly positive experience. I knew I made a good decision in coming to Illinois. Football and academics went well. I came home for Thanksgiving break and again for semester break, which lasted four weeks. I returned to Illinois my second semester in January. That is when football winter conditioning started, which was very intense. Two hours a day, four days a week, we went to the

"Great West Hall" of the stadium, where the coaches had a weight room and a large open space for indoor running and conditioning drills. We spent two days weight lifting, and two days running and agility drills each week until spring football practices began.

Spring football practice ran four days a week for five weeks (currently only 15 practices are allowed). On the last Saturday, we had the big orange and blue intra squad scrimmage which was held in the stadium and open to the public.

I made some good friends. Besides Dan Beaver and Dave, there was a very interesting character and freshman by the name of Patrick Nipote. He was from a catholic school in Des Moines, Iowa. Pat was a golden-gloves junior boxing champion for the state of Iowa, had karate background, and was All-State in football and track. He was a very gifted athlete and one of two or three on the football team with a handlebar mustache. He was a huge fan of the 50's, Elvis Presley and played the drums. He owned a '57 Chevy, which he rebuilt completely and stored back home in Iowa. Pat was a very gregarious guy. He had a high school sweetheart, Andrea, back home in Des Moines. When he arrived his freshman year to the U of I, he reported as a fullback. So, I had close friends on the foot-ball team and we always found something to do on the weekends.

During spring football, I had pretty good success, although there was a lot of talent ahead of me at my position: James and Larry came from the same high school in New York and were known as the "touchdown twins." "Fuzzy" from Gary, Indiana, started as a freshman the previous fall on the varsity. Dave, another player named Mike, a Champaign Central High School graduate, and I were all fighting it out for that swing-back position, although Fuzzy had the inside track.

I felt good and enjoyed the football program. I was looking forward to working out in the summer, becoming stronger and faster and reporting back in August for my sophomore year. It was just a few months ago, I sat on the locker room bench feeling depressed and wondering if I made the right choice. Now I had connection and purpose for being on this campus. It was a busy and full life. It has been said that a student-athlete actually has two jobs. Going to classes and studies are primary, but practicing and playing football is another year-long full-time job. It is a lot of work, but highly fulfilling.

My college life was not all football and classes. I purchased a guitar and taught myself to play. I picked up a chord book and learned some Neil Diamond tunes. Dan Beaver and I would play basketball until 6 o'clock then get back to the dorms in time to eat dinner and study a little. Then we would go back to play more basketball for another hour or two. That was the time where my basketball skills dramatically improved. I actually became pretty good at it.

Coming back to the Detroit area for the summer between my freshman and sophomore year was very rewarding. I worked out at my high school, lifted weights, played basketball, and went to work for my stepfather selling steel.

One of the more awkward moments of the summer occurred when somehow I had a date to attend a Neil Diamond concert with two different girls. Of course, I only had two tickets for one night. I had a regular main girlfriend, Kathy, but I thought we broke off our relationship and I hadn't seen her for three or four weeks, so when I didn't hear from her regarding the concert, I asked another girl to attend. A few days before the concert, Kathy decided to go with me. I had to act quickly. I took Kathy to the concert on the original night and bought tickets for the second night and took the other girl. I felt like Rick Nelson in the old Ozzie and Harriet TV show. I don't think the girls caught on that I went twice with two different dates.

By early August, I was ready to go back for my sophomore year at the University of Illinois and go through the routine again of reporting to football practice double sessions. I was a little bit bigger, faster and stronger. I was probably up to about 170 pounds. I was down to 4.55 seconds in the 40-yard dash, which is in the top 5 or 10 on the team. I was third on the depth chart for swing-back position on the varsity behind Fuzzy and one of the "touchdown twins".

I showed great improvement. I thought I was vying for third, maybe second-string position on varsity due to injuries and/or attrition of other players. After two weeks into double sessions the coach moved a freshman ahead of me and I was real upset. I sat and talked with the coaches about it. They tried to soothe my conscious and ego, to no avail. I was really upset and disappointed and decided to use my red-shirt year and not play on the field for varsity-reserve games and retain eligibility for a fifth year option.

I had a lot of free time on my hands, so I practiced guitar and on alternate weekends, visited my girlfriend (yes, I was back steady with my original sweetheart), who decided to attend Western Michigan University in Kalamazoo, Michigan. I continued to play a lot of basketball at the campus recreation building basketball courts.

When I came back from semester break, I went full-bore into winter conditioning. When spring ball ended, the coaching staff approached me and asked if I wanted to move to defense. I reported back in the fall of my junior year (August 1975) as a defensive back. I was third on the depth chart, so I got to play on the varsity reserve team and had some good games. In a home junior varsity (JV) game against Notre Dame, I had a couple interceptions and a long punt return and we won. It was very gratifying to beat one of the top programs in the country even though it was on the JV level with only 300 people in a stadium that seats 70,000 fans.

III.

INFORMED DECISION

In the fall of 1975, I was living in The Granada House on the corner of Fourth and Chalmers. Campus lore said publisher Hugh Hefner and parody folk singer Allen Sherman lived there when they attended the University of Illinois. That October, my sister Sheryl and her husband stopped in Champaign while driving out west during their honeymoon and stayed in my room. I, ahem, slept elsewhere.

In early November, Pat Nipote, who was living in the apartment next to me, asked if he could sleep in my apartment. I asked why he didn't want to continue living with Andrea, his girlfriend. He told me he became a Christian, was water baptized earlier that month and wanted to wait until his wedding in December to sleep with her. I said, "You're crazy, but OK, stay with me".

I had this tiny room and he moved his single bed in with mine. We were cramped. One night, when we were both sleeping, I rolled over and smacked him with my forearm over the bridge of his nose, which had been broken a short time earlier during football practice. The next day I was telling the story to some friends and as I demonstrated the action, I smacked Pat in the nose again! The way Pat tells this story, I was the one who broke his nose in football practice (I'm not so sure of this since we both played defense) and therefore, he claims I broke his nose three times within 24 hours!

Earlier in the semester, I was invited to Fellowship of Christian Athletes (FCA) meetings on Wednesday evenings. Some of my football friends attended and I decided to check it out. The only previous time I was confronted with the gospel was with Dan Beaver. I had a pleasant experience during my sophomore year when Dan asked me to join him during an overnight high school Christian youth group retreat and talk about my Jewish heritage and upbringing.

FCA, a Christian bible-study, was lead by a local pastor, Jerry Gibson. Both male and female Illinois athletes attended from all walks of life, although meetings were open to non-athletes as well. Jerry spoke of Jesus as the Jewish Messiah and savior for all mankind.

Although I hadn't given the topic much thought since attending yeshiva, the subject of the Messiah was of special interest to me. As I recall, the rabbis had differing theories describing the Messiah as a person, place, thing or event. While attending FCA meetings, combining the interest other people showed in my Judaism and talking about Jesus as the Jewish Messiah led me to start reading a bible that was given to me. I read the New Testament and the Hebrew bible.

I read the prophecies from the Hebrew bible (the Tenach) about the Jewish Messiah with great interest. I was attending the meetings weekly, and hanging out with "born again" Christian friends. There was an excitement about them and the message they wanted to share. Many were very bold and spoke out to people on the campus Quad and street corners about their faith, forgiveness of sins and their changed lives.

Part of my research about Jesus included speaking to the local rabbi. He is a Polish-born Holocaust survivor and highly respected in the Jewish community locally, nationally and internationally. Several years later, he had the honor to be chosen to lead the newly reopened synagogue in East Berlin. We spoke about who Jesus was and how the Jewish leadership today viewed him. The Rabbi told me there was kind of a metamorphosis of thought, whereby for a long while the Jews believed Jesus didn't exist, then he was a teacher and now it is common for some to believe Jesus was a Jewish prophet. For clarification, I asked if the Jews today realize Jesus is Jewish and a leader of his time. He told me some Jewish people believe there are too many historical contexts to refute the claim.

Another topic we covered was why the Jews receive unfair criticism for being called Christ killers. The Rabbi was adamant that the Jews did not kill Jesus, saying it was a Roman plot to have him killed. That statement was thought provoking and I wanted to see historical citation for it. He told me to read among other resources, the Christian bible, which I did.

45

I asked him, "Who or what is the Messiah for the Jewish people?" He told me there are several possibilities. The Rabbi offered that we could live in messianic times, whereby the Jews and Israel would have military peace. Or, perhaps a messianic event, such as a war could change the scope of the political landscape. None of the conjectures he offered revolved around a single person who is to be killed and therefore sacrificed for sins of all mankind.

The Rabbi posed a question to me: "Do you stop being a Jew if you believe Jesus is the Messiah?" This led me to a closer look at my beliefs. Traditional thought states that if a Jew believes in a god or gods other than the God of Abraham, Isaac and Jacob, he is no longer a Jew. I decided to start from the beginning. I researched the Torah to find out from the source, from God's own heart, what he says about Himself and the Jewish Messiah. The first thing I noticed in the first chapter of the bible is "Elohim", the Hebrew word for God is plural not singular. As in "Let *us* (Elohim) make man in our image, after *our* likeness" (Genesis 1:26). Why does the Tenach state "our" and not "his" image. Wouldn't it make more sense that God created man in his image? This, of course, leads to the discussion of the Trinity; the Father, Son and Holy Spirit. How can the Jewish monotheistic faith believing in the One and only, true and living God be three? Do Christians believe in three gods? The most famous prayer a Jew can recite is the "Shema". "Hear O Israel, the Lord is our God, the Lord is one". Surprisingly, the Hebrew word for God (eloheynu) in this passage is a plural or compound unity.

The Hebrew word for one, "echad" is one made of many parts. The Hebrew 'yachid' is an absolute and indivisible "one" and is never used in the bible to describe God. Every time God's name is mentioned, whether it is "elohim", "adonai" or "el shaddai", it is in the plural not singular form.

Secondly, God the Father and God the Spirit are simpler concepts for me to comprehend. However, God as a man, a son who would live and then die for the sins of mankind, is a concept where deeper research was needed.

God is the Creator or Father of Creation. In the Hebrew bible, Isaiah 64:8 reads, "But now, O LORD, You are our Father, We are the clay, and You our potter; And all of us are the work of Your hand." Chapter 43, verse 15 in Isaiah states, "I am the Lord, your Holy One, the Creator of Israel, and your King." One of the messianic prophecies states "He will cry to Me, 'You are my Father, My God, and the rock of my salvation. I also shall make him My first-born, The highest of the kings of the earth." (Psalm 89:26-27). There is not much dispute that God the Father is our Creator.

Genesis chapter 1 says "the Spirit of God moving upon the surface of the waters." Job said during his trials, 'the Spirit of God has made me" (Job 33:4). The Hebrew bible teaches that kings, prophets and priests had the Spirit of God upon to help them perform their services. We clearly see God is one but still is described in the bible in different ways.

There are other manifestations of God in the bible. Who appeared with Shadrach, Mishach and Abednego in the seven times heated furnace? Even Nebuchadnezzar, the King who doomed the three men to their fiery fate, exclaimed it was an angel or the son of God. God appeared to Moses in the fashion of a burning bush. If God can appear in these manners, why can't the one and only true and living God come to earth as the Son of God, the Messiah? Over the centuries, God has manifested himself in many ways. Therefore, the Christian view of the Tri-Unity of God is not in direct conflict with the Hebrew bible.

Is Jesus Jewish? If he is the Messiah he would have to be Jewish. In another predictive verse, written by the Jewish prophet Isaiah, it is written, "For a child will born to **us**, a son will be given to **us**: and the government will rest upon his shoulders; and his name shall be called Wonderful Counselor, Mighty God, the Eternal Father, the Prince of Peace." (Isaiah 9:6). The **'us"** are the people of Isaiah, the Hebrew nation! Therefore, the Son is Jewish.

What is the purpose of the Son, the Messiah? There are a string of scripture verses in the Hebrew bible, prophecies really, indicating the coming of the Messiah. One who is to be born, live amongst his people and die for the sins of mankind.

Read the Hebrew prophet Isaiah, Chapter 53 (emphases mine):

The Suffering Servant

1 Who has believed our message? And to whom has the arm of the LORD been revealed?

2 For He grew up before Him like a tender shoot, and like a root out of parched ground; He has no *stately* form or majesty that we should look upon Him, nor appearance that we should be attracted to Him.

3 He was despised and forsaken of men, a man of sorrows and acquainted with grief; and like one from whom men hide their face, He was despised; and we did not esteem Him.

4 Surely our griefs He Himself bore, and our sorrows He carried; yet we ourselves esteemed Him stricken, smitten of God, and afflicted.

5 *But he was pierced through for our transgressions, he was crushed for our iniquities; the chastening for our well-being fell upon Him; and by His scourging we are healed.*

6 *All we like sheep have gone astray; each of us has turned to his own way; but the Lord has caused the iniquity of us all to fall upon Him.*

7 He was oppressed, and He was afflicted, yet He did not open His mouth; like a lamb that is led to slaughter and like a sheep that is silent before its shearers, so he did not open His mouth.

8 By oppression and judgment he was taken away; and as for his generation, who considered that he was cut off out of the land of the living for the transgression of my people to whom the stroke was due?

9 His grave was assigned with wicked men, yet He was a rich man in his death; because He had done no violence, nor was there was any deceit in his mouth.

10 *But the Lord was pleased to crush Him; putting Him to grief: If He would render Himself as a guilt offering, He will see His offspring, He will prolong His days, and the good pleasure of the Lord will prosper in His hand.*

11 *As a result of the anguish of his soul, He will see it and be satisfied: by His knowledge of the Righteous One, my righteous servant will justify many; as He will bear their iniquities.*

12 *Therefore will I allot him a portion with the great, and He will divide the booty with the strong; because he poured Himself out to death, and He was numbered with the transgressors:* **yet He Himself bore the sin of many, and interceded for the transgressors.**

Sin; now there is a word that isn't spoken much. Who among us would admit to sin? Perhaps we realize that we do wrong to other people, but do we transgress against God? Will we admit our unbelief? I am convinced the key to believing and following God is to humble ourselves before Him. In this day and age, are we willing to put God's commandments ahead of out own needs and desires? Forgiveness of sins was so important; God set a method for all the

Jewish people to receive it. Leviticus chapter 16:29-34 reveals to us that once a year, the High Priest from the tribe of Levi dresses appropriately, goes into the Holy of Holies within the Temple in Jerusalem, sacrifices a lamb without any blemish and if God is pleased the High Priest is not killed and goes out to the people. Because life is in the blood, the lamb is a propitiation for the sins of the people. Sin is so disgusting to God, something has to be killed and blood must be shed each year. This is the holiest day in the Jewish calendar and is called Yom Kippur, the Day of Atonement. To be forgiven of sins and having a clean conscience provides for an individual relationship with God the Father and entrance into eternity – heaven.

Nowadays, a Jew cannot receive forgiveness from God using the Torah principles. There is no lineage to the Levite and High Priest; no Temple and even the sacrificing of animals are repugnant to the modern Jew. Therefore, there is little to connect us to the original terms of Yom Kippur (Day of Atonement). Many Jews today believe in a progressive revelation, that going to shul (synagogue) while praying and fasting on Yom Kippur is enough to receive forgiveness. To many Jews this method is enough to satisfy their need for forgiveness. I believe this practice to be biblically unsound. God has His own revealed progressive revelation. As stated in Isaiah, He sent his own son, Yeshua, to be our propitiation for sins, ONCE AND FOR ALL TIME. We are forgiven in the sight of God. What greater news is there than this!

What about the bible? The Hebrew bible or Torah is the basis of history and beliefs for the Jewish people. The Christian bible includes both the New Testament and the Hebrew bible. The two cannot be separated, for the New Testament or New Covenant is based on the writings of the Hebrew bible. The lineage of Jesus, prophesies pertaining to the coming Messiah, and the Kingdom of Heaven are interrelated. When I compare the two books, I notice direct links.

Like a jigsaw puzzle, the pieces started to come together for me. Although I could see throughout the Tenach there was to be a "saving" Messiah, how do we know Jesus fits the bill? I read the Christian bible, the New Testament, closely and intensely and the message was clear. Jesus, the Messiah, son of Joseph and Mary, fulfilled the Hebrew prophecies and is the Savior not only for the Jewish people but for the whole world. The four Gospels, The book of the Acts of the Holy Spirit and the Book of Romans attest to His lineage, Godship and Savior role for all humanity.

There is another Christian Jewish dilemma. Over the centuries, so-called Christians in the name of God put Jews to death. Let us compare those "christian" actions to the scriptures. According to the New Testament, Jesus is Jewish. He was a teacher and a prophet. He taught many things; including the greatest commandment "love God and love others as you would have them love you." We know it as the "Golden Rule". I do not believe that people acting in the name of "god," killing off the Jews, were truly Christians. They were acting on personal agendas, politics and ignorance. The Jesus I have learned about is against prejudice, bias and racism. If He is truly the Son of Man and the Son of God, then His teachings should be carried out by people for the sake of the kingdom of God, not the kingdom of man.

This reasoning holds for the holocaust. Adolph Hitler was a demented dictator. His final solution was racism in its most grotesque form. His religion, whatever it was, had nothing to do with his plan to exterminate the Jewish race. His actions and the actions of Nazis had nothing to do with the true beliefs of the Christian religion. I am very proud of the Germans who have taken steps, over the years, to apologize for the atrocities taken in the name of their beloved Deutschland.

What about the Jews as Christ-killers? Although I can see a logical implication, biblically this isn't the whole story. Calling Jews "Christ-killers" implies we actually killed their Christ, the King of Kings. As I read scripture, the prophets foretold the death of the Messiah at the hands of His own people for an eternal purpose. The story of the Messiah is for Him to live and die and raise again from death so each man and woman can be forgiven for their sins once and for all time. So, as the Passover lamb without any blame, Jesus had to die. *He gave up his life freely* so He could rise from the dead and lead us to forgiveness and eternal life. It is a sad story with a wonderful ending. So, although it is true the Jewish leaders plotted the death of one of their own, it was the Romans who carried out the sentence, flogged and killed Him as a traitor to the Roman Empire. In a very real sense, it was the sins of all mankind not merely the plotting of the Jews or the Roman crucifixion that lead to the death of Jesus. He is the sacrificial lamb who willingly followed the road of sorrows. This is the New Covenant, the Gospel.

So let us go back to the question the rabbi posed to me: can a Jew still be a Jew and a Christian? My answer, after careful research is: yes. It is not a matter of being one or the other. A Jewish believer simply believes in the Messiah. I understand that in Jewish tradition, if you leave the faith for another you are no longer considered Jewish. Some Jewish families go as far as to have a funeral for their "dead" child. Like many rules, finding the Messiah seems to be an exception to me. Jesus was Jewish, he fulfilled the prophecies of the Hebrew bible and all the first believers in the religion were Jews. The Christian bible says the gospel should be shared first to the Jew and then to the nations. Why is there such a foundation of the Christian religion to the Jews? Because Christianity is a Jewish religion! Don't get me wrong, I don't necessarily mean that all believers in Jesus should observe Jewish traditions. The Christian faith is based in Jewish roots and Jews do not give up their own roots by believing in Yeshua. "Make up your mind", call out the skeptics. I believe it is not a matter of vacillating between two different religions. It is a continuum. For Abraham, it was a matter of faith in one God. With Moses, there was a deliverance out of Egyptian bondage and the bringing forth of the written law. Jesus is the New Covenant with eternal salvation for all. One God, one faith, one religion.

For example, the evening Jesus celebrated with His disciples, commonly known as the Last Supper, is actually Passover (Pesach). Jesus took the two main symbolic elements, matzo and wine and gave them a second, eternal meaning. Originally, in the Passover Seder, matzo signified the Hebrews leaving Egypt in haste and the wine represents the lambs' blood on the doorways where the angel of death passed over the homes. In a somber foretelling of the next day's events, the unleavened bread symbolizes the sacrificial sinless life of Jesus and the wine symbolically became His blood, which will be poured in His ensuing death. Jesus became the Paschal (Passover) Lamb.

Most Jews are Jewish by race and culture as well as religion. The Jewish race was founded by Abraham. His lineage is depicted in the bible as "begats" throughout history. The Jewish lineage of Jesus is tracked in the bible. Religious Jews are Jews because they believe in the one and only, true and living God. Deuteronomy 6:4 is the religious battle cry of the Jews: "Hear O Israel, the Lord is God the Lord is One!" I do not believe any less in this scripture than before I became a believer in Jesus as the Messiah. The current tradition in Judaism is that if the mother is Jewish then her children are Jewish (in spite of the precedent set by biblical patriarchal lineage). This is regardless of their religious belief. This tradition also holds in the Israeli Courts of Law. Being Jewish can also apply to citizenship. So, the only thing keeping me from continuing as a Jew while a Christian is if I left my faith. My mother is Jewish and Jesus is Jewish, therefore I am still Jewish.

One of the great debates in Judaism is about the Messiah. In brief, some believe it to be a system of government, to others a leader to help with everyday needs of the people. I adhere to the scripture written in Isaiah 53 that He is the Lamb of God to be killed for the remission of our sins and have eternal life.

Yeshua is more than research or a belief system. A person can have a personal relationship with Him through the Holy Spirit. The Holy Spirit (Ruach Hakodesh) dwells within his followers as promised by the Hebrew prophets. Rabbis believe that the Holy Spirit is an attribute of God that provides inspiration, not a separate division within the Tri-Unity of the Godhead. The Holy Scriptures in Joel chapter 2 and Ezekiel chapter 36 reveals the promise of the Holy Spirit for all mankind. No longer is God's Spirit only for priests, prophets and kings. Read these passages and perhaps you will be amazed as I.

Book of Joel chapter 2:

27 *"Thus you will know that I am in the midst of Israel, And that I am the LORD your God,*

And there is no other; And My people will never be put to shame.

28 *"It will come about after this that I will pour out My Spirit on all mankind;*

And your sons and daughters will prophesy, Your old men will dream dreams, Your young men will see visions.

[29] *"Even on the male and female servants I will pour out My Spirit in those days.*

[30] *"I will display wonders in the sky and on the earth, Blood, fire and columns of smoke.*

[31] *"The sun will be turned into darkness And the moon into blood before the great and awesome day of the LORD comes.*

[32] *"And it will come about that whoever calls on the name of the LORD will be delivered; For on Mount Zion and in Jerusalem There will be those who escape, as the LORD has said, even among the survivors whom the LORD calls.*

Book of Ezekiel chapter 36:

[24] *"For I will take you from the nations, gather you from all the lands and bring you into your own land.*

[25] *"Then I will sprinkle clean water on you, and you will be clean; I will cleanse you from all your filthiness and from all your idols.*

[26] *"Moreover, I will give you a new heart and put a new spirit within you; and I will remove the heart of stone from your flesh and give you a heart of flesh.*

[27] *"I will put My Spirit within you and cause you to walk in My statutes and you will be careful to observe My ordinances.*

IV.

RIVER OF SEPARATION

O n Wednesday, April 28, 1976, the weekly FCA meeting was held in the Campus YMCA building. Afterwards, a group of about 12 people gathered at a house Pat and Andy Nipote (they were married by now) were house-sitting. It was a time for snacks, visiting and doing some homework.

Kirk, who was captain of the football team in the late 60's and migrated back to Champaign earlier that month, was sitting at the dining room table and I joined him. We discussed my journey and research regarding the Messiah. We read through several chapters of the Book of Romans (written by Saul, a Jew, later known as Paul) in the New Testament. What a wonderful treatise on the difference between the Law and Grace; the difference between believing with your heart and doing good deeds. Even in Chapter 4, Abraham is recognized as a man of faith even unto righteousness before his circumcision (rite of a Jewish man). Then the kicker: "Therefore, having been justified by faith, we have peace with God through our Lord Jesus Christ" (Romans 5:1). I was convinced Jesus is the Jewish messiah.

Kirk then asked the question I heard numerous times in the previous eight months: "What prevents you from accepting Jesus as your Savior?" This time I had no excuse, only a calming peace came over me. "Nothing" I said. Kirk said, "Let's pray." I prayed and accepted into my mind and my heart Jesus as the Messiah and my personal Savior.

This was the beginning of a very exciting time in the house for me and the others. I had finally overcome any objections. I had answers to my questions and my heart was ready to accept Jesus as the Christ – the Jewish Messiah.

Jesus the Messiah: you don't hear that phrase in Jewish circles. What had I gotten myself into? A nice Jewish boy from Detroit, an Illinois football player, should not become a Christian...or should he? There were so many obstacles to overcome, both real and imagined. Throughout history, the Jews have been the minority and continually bullied. They faced prosecutions and persecutions. Yet, here I opened my life and heart to the God of the Jews. Jesus came to earth to minister to the needs of the people, live a perfect life, died for the sins of all mankind and rose from the dead so we can all live in eternity. It is God's plan and I accept it wholeheartedly.

There were several things going on at the house at the same time. There were three or four people in the garage playing the piano and singing. Another small group was in the living room praying for special needs and counseling one another using the bible. And there were Kirk and I, sitting at the dining room table, praying for Jesus to enter my life.

All of a sudden there was a rush of emotion over me and an air of festivity fell on the room. I felt the presence of God, His Holy Spirit upon us. I never felt anything like it before. It was better than scoring the winning touchdown or a kiss on a first date. I felt something PERSONAL and ETERNAL. The promises of God are true. Everyone converged into the dining room without any spoken direction. There was so much anticipation over the months that I would accept the Gospel of Jesus, everyone poured his or her heart open with joy to the Lord. Everyone started singing to God; songs of joy and celebration. I didn't know the words to the songs, but there was a massive amount of passion for God in the room. After so much intellectual research of the Gospel, I actually felt the presence of a Greater Being! So many people had so much impact on my life and waiting for me to step forward and it took a stranger to ask the question unfettered. Some thought I may face serious repercussion from my family for this decision, but all I knew is that the Gospel, the Good News, is the truth.

It was midnight before I went to my apartment on Clark Street in Champaign. It was a quaint building; only a couple years old and very clean. Not long after I got home, I received a phone call from Jerry Gibson who was the sponsor of the campus FCA group and pastor at a local church in Urbana. He wanted to know if I wanted to get water baptized. I had to give it some thought because I knew through my studies of the bible that this was an event not to be taken lightly. I told him to give me some time to think about it. As I lay in my bed too awake to sleep, I thought about my new commitment to Jesus the Christ or as He known in Hebrew ...Yeshua Hamoshiach.

I went to class the next day, but could scarcely concentrate. All I could think about was what I had done the previous night and how God met me. What a great feeling. But even more than that was the knowledge my decision was right. I decided to get water baptized and that to delay would be wrong. It is a step of faith in a believer's life and a sign of obedience to God's Word. Water had been used for centuries before Jesus time on earth as a symbol of cleansing impurities in the lives of Jews. There was a Mikva, a water pool for such purposes, near my yeshivah. Jesus was water baptized, as He said to "fulfill all righteousness". The bible New Covenant says "believe and be baptized". So, I did.

I arrived at the church at 7 p.m. sharp. There was time of prayer and singing of psalms and hymns. Four people including myself were scheduled to be water baptized. Minister Jerry Gibson presided over the event and apparently found the others who wanted to be baptized. I didn't know them, but the more the merrier. There were about twenty people in the audience to witness the baptisms including some people very close to me were in attendance. A friend from the football team, Mark, did the honors of taking us into the waters one at a time. After each of us were immersed in the water and dried off and in new clothes, we had a time of prayer and worshipping God. Then, lo and behold, three people asked to be baptized. One prayed on the spot to become a believer and the other two re-dedicated their lives to Christ. One of the re-dedicators was Kirk, the person who prayed with me to accept Jesus as my Savior the night before. I soon discovered that the reason Kirk returned to Illinois was in part, to try to find God more fully in his own life. So, we prayed some more, Mark baptized them and then we sang praises to God some more.

We decided to go to Jerry's house to reflect and relax and have some refreshments. Jerry's wife, Normadeene, is a very kind and gentle lady and greeted about ten of us with open arms. We had fun talking, visiting and telling tales of our lives in general and the evening events. Then, the phone rang. Another attendee of the early evening event wanted to get baptized. So, we loaded up our vehicles and headed back to the church. It turned out that three more people wanted to get baptized. So, we prayed, sang some songs (are you noticing a pattern here) and had three more baptisms. All told, we had 10 people following Jesus' example of water baptism. What a great night!

The events of those twenty four hours were a lot to handle; so much emotion, so much praise to God and so much happiness. Can it be this way everyday in God's love?

One of the harsh realities of a Jew becoming a Christian is that different beliefs can be tolerated by the Jews, but action by a Jew, in a direction away from the Jewish beliefs, such as baptism, appears to be a rejection of Judaism. This is a real separation. Nothing magical physically happens in the water, but nevertheless it is a red-letter action stating, "I have made a commitment to my faith in God."

Then, I had another decision to make. How would I tell my parents, my family and my friends? Frankly, I chickened out. A month after committing to my new found faith, I went home for the summer and behaved as though nothing happened back on campus. I continued to date my longtime girlfriend, Kathy, and spent the summer working part time jobs and vacationing in central Michigan. It was the United States Bicentennial and I enjoyed the festivities in Detroit on the river and around the state. I spent a large amount of my time at my high school lifting weights and playing basketball to stay in shape for football.

A friend told me a few months ago "Don't tell people what to do. Tell them who God is". The people in our campus bible study did just that. During the fall of 1975 and spring of 1976, many college students were receiving and believing the salvation message and their lives were changed. People who were living in the streets and doing drugs stopped their old lifestyle and became new people in Christ. Second Corinthians Chapter 5 verse 17 reads: "Therefore, if any man is in Christ, he is a new creature; the old things pass away; behold, new things have come." The scriptures, by the Spirit of God, became alive in people.

I returned to campus in August and some changes were happening with the athletes' connection to FCA. Some of the student leaders were sensing a break was needed to have a stronger walk with God. FCA met just once a week and many of the group wanted to gather more frequently. The leaders of the young group also believed that gifts from the Holy Spirit such as healing and prophesy continue to be used today. This was new stuff for me, but I decided to go with the flow. It was exciting to preach on the quad and have our own bible study in the dorms. Every Monday night, there were about 30 students reading and studying the bible together. The emphasis was learning about salvation, the life of Jesus and how we can behave in a more pious manner. There was a lot of talk about the infilling of the Holy Spirit. In the Hebrew bible it is taught that only kings, priests and prophets had the Spirit upon them. In the New Covenant, all believers can have the Holy Spirit (Hebrew: Ruach Hakodesh) living in them and directing their life. The Holy Spirit empowers people to follow God, understand the word of God (the bible) and change your life. See what John the Baptist says in Matthew 3:11, Mark 1:8, Luke 3:16, John 1:33. Also, read the whole book of ACTS.

Matthew 3:11: "As for me I baptize you with water for repentance, but he that is coming after me is mightier than I, and I am not fit to remove His sandals: He will baptize you with the Holy Spirit and fire."

Mark 1:7-8: 'And he was preaching and saying, after me One is coming that is mightier than I. I baptized you with water; but he will baptize you in the Holy Spirit."

Luke 3:16: "John answered and said to them all, as for me I baptize you with water; but One is coming who is mightier than I, and I am not fit to stoop down and untie the thong of His sandals. He will baptize you in the Holy Spirit and fire."

John 1:33: "And I did not recognize Him: but he who sent me to baptize in water, said to me, He upon whom you see the Spirit descending, and remaining upon him, this is the One that baptizes in the Holy Spirit."

Three young men emerged from the group as leaders: Steve Schraeder, Doug Keller and Patrick Nipote. Steve didn't attend the university, but he was only a couple years older than the rest of us, a very talented singer, musician and public speaker. He played piano, keyboards and did a great impression of Elton John and Billy Joel. He became a Christian a few years earlier in the Chicago suburbs and was married with a young son. His intention was to be part of a campus Christian ministry. Doug was one of my teammates who was a year ahead of me. He was a gifted athlete. At 6-3, 250 pounds, Doug was physically imposing. He was charismatic and has strong of personality. He lettered in both football and baseball at Illinois and hailed from New Jersey. Pat, as mentioned earlier, was a teammate and former roommate. These were young men who influenced others in very unique ways and had strong leadership abilities.

Steve was dynamic and had a magnetic personality. He could talk to anyone at any time on almost any topic. He had an air of the theatrical, meaning he didn't mind being the center of attention and was never flustered in front of a crowd. Doug was a leader by example. He worked very hard in practice and in games and teammates would want to do better because of Doug's efforts. Patrick has a compassionate nature. He married his high school sweetheart and had a heart for people who never quite get the attention they deserve. All three were bright, articulate and had a heart to follow God.

I was eager to start football again. I love the first week of practice: getting into uniform and working hard to obtain playing time. Football is a great sport, a true team sport. Every play, every snap from center depends on all eleven men executing perfectly for a great play to occur. Of course, the eleven men on the other side of the ball are trying to accomplish the same goal. It is a battle every time those men come to the line of scrimmage.

During one of the early practices, I ran smack into a fullback about 30 pounds heavier than me. BOOM! I was knocked unconscious and felt myself slowly drifting to the ground. I missed seven days of practice, which is devastating to earn a starting position. I reported to camp solidly on second team and came back from my injury as a third team player.

The 1976 season didn't progress as well for the team as a whole, but at least I got to see some action during games. I wasn't a starter, but I did play on "suicide" or specialty teams in a few games. Mainly, I was the wedge-buster on the kickoff team. The coaches wanted to utilize my speed, so I ran down the field and threw my body across as many blockers as possible in front of the opposing kick returner. This strategy is used to open up the field for my teammates to make the tackle. I was happy to oblige.

Before the final game of the season against Northwestern University, the athletic director fired our head coach Bob Blackman. The players were very upset. We took it as a reflection of our own abilities as opposed to the coaches' efforts. We took it out on the Wildcats and shut them out. This led to a new regime coming in. The athletic director hired University of Michigan Defensive Coordinator, Gary Moeller. On paper, it looked like a good hire with all the success Michigan had since Bo Schembechler took over that program. I stuck it out during spring ball and impressed the staff enough to finish as a first team defensive back. Coach Moeller put together a great staff. Lloyd Carr, now retired head football coach at Michigan, was our defensive backs coach. Several others on the staff are still coaching, some as head coaches.

There were some changes to the bible study group during the 1976-77 academic year. We decided to take on a different identity instead of being referred to as "the dorm bible study". Officially, we became "Rescue Shop" after a song written by one of our attendees. Commonly we were known as the "No Name Fellowship". We became very conservative in our biblical thinking on several issues and took the bible highly literal. We were still evangelistic, but moving towards deeper understanding of God (a holiness doctrine) and learning how to follow His direction daily as individuals and as a group. We moved our meeting place from a dormitory to a church in Urbana. They let us use it at no charge on Friday nights. This worked well since most of the attendees were college students and we didn't want to get up early on Sunday mornings to attend meetings. We didn't call it going to church, but, rather, "attending fellowship meetings". By the early summer 1977, we had elders – Steve, Patrick and Jerry Hastings. It was strange to call them elders since they were basically the same age as me. Older Christian men in the community tried to convince us to attend traditional churches, but our leaders felt it necessary for this new movement of God to work on its own. Doug Keller would have been chosen as one of the original elders, but he was drafted by the Cleveland Browns professional football team and would be away for extensive periods of time.

By this time, I was not the only Jewish believer of Jesus' teachings on campus. We heard of a mini explosion of Jews accepting Jesus in America and around the world during this period of time and our campus was a local link to the Jewish people becoming new believers in Jesus.

Friday evenings were exciting and we looked forward to the group meetings. We spent time in prayer, singing worship songs to Jesus and opened it up for anyone to share from their bible or experiences. It was done in reverence to show our appreciation for God and what He had done for each of us. We had some talented music composers. Linn Laurence wrote several worship and praise songs that we adopted. She also found an old hymn, "Camel Train", which she sung at several local weddings; including mine. The song is about the biblical marriage between Isaac and Rebekkah as arranged by Abraham's servant, Eliezer. It also foreshadows God sending his Son for his bride, the church. The chorus goes like this:

Oh, get ready, evening shadows fall.
Don't you hear the Eliezer call?
For there's going to be a wedding, our joy will soon begin;
In the evening when the camel train comes in.

During the summer of 1976 Doug Keller's hard work paid off and was picked as a 10th round draft choice by the Cleveland Browns as an offensive tackle and signed an NFL contract. However, during summer practices, with the professional team, he injured his knee, had surgery and underwent rehabilitation for a year. When he reported back to the Browns in July of 1977, he failed the physical. This news affected Doug deeply and I believe this to be a major event for the fellowship. During the year of his rehab, things became more intense. Doug was attending classes, living off his football paycheck and rehabbing his knee. He spent a lot of time reading the bible, fasting, and praying. He became very strong in his beliefs. It was then that Doug became an elder in the fellowship. Although we continued to have an open format in the meetings, Doug would give a teaching to finish virtually every meeting. He and Steve Schraeder were beginning to be the dominant speakers in the group.

We continued to be evangelistic in our intent. It was very important to us to share the gospel anywhere and anytime. A minority of people within the group preached a type of "hell, fire and brimstone" gospel to students on campus. This was hard for me to grasp because I came to know the Lord through His love, patience and movement of His Spirit. Doug posted a bible passage on the front door of his apartment: "Repent or perish". Some people in the group thought it was cool to be so overt with his strong and harsh beliefs.

In May 1976, about a month after I became a born again Christian, a man named Arthur Katz came to a local church to speak. He is a Jewish man who came to the knowledge of Jesus as his Messiah while searching spiritual things as a professor at University of California at Berkley. He wrote a book, "Ben Israel, the Odyssey of a Modern Jew" that is worth the read. He is extremely intelligent and used an extensive vocabulary. He had an aura about him that made you want to learn more about Jesus. He spoke for an hour and finished with a prayer. As a result of this visit, Doug and Steve became fast friends with Art and the fellowship group planned several trips to his ministry location in central Minnesota. There were men who had oversight of Ben Israel Ministries and Camp Dominion in Minnesota. There were several families and some single people who lived in this community and lived off the land and earned money as a camp for Christian believers holding seminars and retreats. Art also traveled the world talking about his Jewish heritage and sharing the gospel of Jesus.

Over the next twenty-four months or so, people from our fellowship would periodically travel to Camp Dominion. We received ministry, prayer and mentorship from their leaders. Camp Dominion was geographically off the beaten path and their doctrine had a "holiness" bent to it.

Each May, the Full Gospel Businessmen International Fellowship (FGBMFI) had a regional convention in Green Lake, Wisconsin. For this particular convention in 1977, our fellowship group was placed in charge of the youth meetings. I'm sure it was an enlightening time for the teenagers as Doug and Steve would tell their testimonies on how they came to know Christ as their Savior. The teens were spellbound. We also had fun and games and entertained the teenagers with live music.

One evening, in the privacy of our cabin, I was sharing my testimony with a local FGBMI leader, Gene, about how I, a Jew, became a believer. It took me about two hours to get through the whole story. He was so impressed he asked me to tell my story in front of the whole convention of about 300 Christian believers. I had never publicly spoke and balked at the offer. Then he said for me to tell the story in 15 minutes. Oh yeah, sure, not only do I need to talk, but do it in a succinct manner?! I thought and prayed about it and the next morning told Gene I would do it. That afternoon, I was announced as a speaker and actually spoke for about 20 minutes and hit the high points on my Jewish upbringing, scriptures and how my friends helped bring me into a relationship with Jesus the Messiah.

After that session, a lady came and introduced me to her friend, a Jewish believer by the name of Joe. I congratulated him and then he relayed an amazing story. He told his lady friend, if a Jewish person would get up in front of the whole convention and confess Jesus as Lord, he would do so himself. Not two minutes later, I was talking on stage. The lesson learned is all you need to do sometimes is just be there, simply show up. God will take care of the rest. Joe wasn't the first person I led to a relationship with Jesus, but it was the first time I introduced someone to Jesus and wasn't even aware of it.

That was the beginning of a very important summer for me. I decided to stay on campus in Illinois instead of moving home for the summer. I wanted to devote myself fulltime to working out for football so I would be better prepared to be a starter in the fall campaign. Although my girlfriend moved to Champaign for the summer we noticed in a very short time it was obvious we were headed in different directions. I was trying to grow close to God and Kathy could not grasp the change in me. We broke off our relationship and she headed back to Michigan. I felt bad for her that she made all this effort to move 400 miles to be near me. After all, it was less than six months earlier that we were considering taking steps toward marriage. But I felt my relationship with God was moving me in a more conservative lifestyle than she and I were used to in the past.

I was coaching a women's softball team in the park district league and another girl soon caught my eye. Most of the women were Christians on the team and Geri is an exceptional lady. The first time I actually met her was to pick her up at her house and take her to a water baptism. As she likes to tell the story, I totally repulsed her. I was a little arrogant, dressed in a wise-guy manner, with my shirt half unbuttoned, and had a racy car; a two-tone blue Dodge Charger Daytona.

Geri wasn't necessarily drawn to athletes as much as the greaser set from her high school days. She was married, briefly, right out of high school, but she had a major life transformation after her divorce, by accepting Jesus into her life in 1973.

Geri started attending fellowship meetings while playing softball for my team. After a few days, I asked her out on a date. It was different. We went to a local pizza place and had a chaperone. His name is Jeff Silverman, who is a Jewish believer in Yeshua and played baseball at Illinois.

Geri and I spent time together and would sit together at fellowship meetings. I was feeling very confident in my place in life; preparing for the football season and reading my bible almost every day. In early July, the fellowship went on another trip to Camp

73

Dominion. Several people "camel-trained" (what we called a vehicle caravan) up to Minnesota. It was a great time of Christian fellowship and breathing the great outdoors. There were special sessions of studying the bible and prayer. During one session we had an opportunity to take communion and Art Katz asked me to lead the service. I did so by reading the first book of Corinthians chapter 11, verse 28 in the bible about each man examining his own heart before taking communion. It was a very touching and poignant moment for the group. We prayed and praised God in song as we each ate pieces of bread and drank a small cup of wine.

Unbeknownst to me, Geri sent out a fleece, a test before God, regarding my seriousness with Him and the relationship between us. I wasn't near her throughout the weekend and she was concerned if our relationship was to grow into the next level. The time of communion revealed a lot. At least she knew I was serious with God.

Earlier in the summer of 1977, I was having great pain in my left shoulder; the one on which I had surgery in high school. The team doctor prescribed a pain-killer, but its effects wore off after a few hours. One Friday evening, my Christian brothers prayed over me, invoking the name and power of Jesus, and I haven't had a moment of pain since. I really thank God for that miracle. I always dreaded taking drugs of any kind, even the legal ones. A person cannot be sure what the side effects might be.

V.

INTERVENTION

Upon my return to Champaign, I decided I needed to tell my parents about becoming a Jewish - Christian believer. It was over a year since my confession of faith and I felt as though the Holy Spirit was politely hounding me to tell the truth to my family. One evening in particular, I couldn't sleep and I felt a Presence in the room. I know it to be the Holy Spirit touching my life in a special way. I knew then I had to stand up for my beliefs. The next day I called my parents and they each got on a phone extension and I tried to get it all out in one sentence. I told them, "I want you to know that I believe in Jesus Christ, Jesus the Messiah, the Son of the God of Abraham, Isaac and Jacob as my Savior." I wanted them to know I was still Jewish, yet believed the Messiah has come. There was a shocked silence for a moment or two and then my step-dad says, "Who is this Abe, Ike and Jake". I didn't know if he was kidding or not but either way, I knew I had my work cut out for myself. Little did I know the chain of events that would occur based on my simple statement. It was the middle of July.

This is about the same time that Doug Keller, the unofficial leader of our bible group, heard he failed his physical with the Cleveland Browns. He worked so hard to get his knee back into shape. What a letdown for him. Soon thereafter, he went on a 40-day fast. He prayed morning, noon and night and his life changed dramatically. He received invitations for speaking engagements all around the country and the world. Within two years, he spoke behind the Iron Curtain, sometimes smuggling bibles.

Geri and I were spending many hours together getting to know each other and falling in love. As a courtesy, I talked to the fellowship elders about our relationship. On August 1, 1977, just weeks after we met, I asked Geri to marry me.

Geri is very special. She is serious about God, loves the outdoors, simple in her ways and beautiful. We were in my apartment and I went down to one knee to pop the question. She promised herself that after her divorce she would only marry a man after God's heart and that I proved myself at Camp Dominion. There was a long silence and she finally spoke. "Yes," was her answer. She asked me why I didn't sit in the meeting with her at Camp Dominion and I told her for that period time I wanted to concentrate on God alone. She was OK with that! Some women would be offended if they were called a distraction. We set a wedding date for December, just five months away.

About this time, I was also wondering if I should continue playing football. I worked really hard on my strength, stamina and speed (I improved to a 4.4 forty). I was reporting back as a starter on defense. However, a scripture came to my mind from I Corinthians 9:27 that reads, "After I have preached to others, I myself should be disqualified." Well, I had shared the gospel to many of my team-mates and felt that mission complete. Football was very important to me but I felt it was time to move on to other things in my life. I asked my Christian friends and they were wholeheartedly behind my decision. The day before the first practice, I went to the stadium to inform the coaches. I sat down with Coach Carr and Coach Parker and explained my decision to them. They were visibly upset, but respected my reasoning for leaving the team. I felt bad to give up one dream, but felt a need to focus on completing my degree and getting married later in the year. Upon reflection, I regret not involving my parents ahead of time and consulting them on the decision.

Geri and I drove to Michigan over Labor Day weekend to meet my family. It was, to say the least, a very awkward visit. It was the first time I saw my family since I told them of my faith in Yeshua, quitting football and bringing home a born again Christian woman to be my bride. Oy vay! My parents privately tried to talk me out of the engagement. After all, I had known Geri only eight weeks before I proposed marriage, planned a wedding for December and they had to get used to other changes in my life. Generally, they never expected me to play college football, however, they were a little upset I quit football, which caught me by surprise. Throughout my athletic career they couldn't understand why I would risk injury and more surgery. Yet, because I decided not to play based on a scripture reference and a move in my heart from God, my parents objected. However, I stood firm and confident in my decisions.

Upon returning to campus, I noticed I wasn't concentrating well in class as my time was taken up working two part-time jobs and going to Christian fellowship meetings. I decided to withdraw from school and re-enter in January so I would be done with my degree from the College of Business in May, 1978.

There were some changes occurring in the fellowship as well. We moved our meetings to Sunday mornings and met at the Jefferson Building in downtown Champaign in their large meeting room. Derek, a preacher from England, became a strong influence to Doug. Based on Derek's teachings the women began to wear head coverings and became very conservative in how they dress. They were not to adorn themselves in any special manner. Jewelry and make up were no longer part of their adornment. Plain jean skirts and button down tops were the norm for the women.

During weekly services, musical praise and worship was very good and the teachings were on topics about growing closer to God and dying to your human nature and taking on the nature of Christ. The congregation was up to about 100 members at this time; mostly college students and young married couples.

Geri and I were planning our wedding for the weekend after final exams in mid-December. When I informed my parents of the date, they said they would be on a cruise and asked to postpone it. I thought their timing to be strange since they usually took their cruise during their wedding anniversary in late December, but, nonetheless, we postponed the wedding six weeks to late January.

On Friday, December 23, 1977, I finished filling out my petition for readmission to the College of Business. My intention was to drop it off at the Student Academic Affairs Office on my way to work. I wanted to get married in January, complete my degree in May and see what my immediate future would hold. I didn't know what direction God was calling me for post graduation. I was a part-time employee at a restaurant chain and perhaps I would move fulltime into management or do something completely different, perhaps in a different state. I wasn't happy I didn't get the degree done on time in December, but I made up my mind to move on and get it done.

I was in the parking lot at my apartment complex with my petition in my hand when I saw two strangers in trench coats approaching from a car. I recall chuckling to myself that these guys looked like some sort of secret agents. One of the men asked me my name and I told him. He then showed me a file and some paperwork telling me I was compelled by a court order to go with them to Chicago. I asked why and they said my Mom wanted to see me. I asked why again and they said she is my temporary guardian and I had to go. I felt relaxed, confident that everything would be OK and my life was not in danger. At that very moment another tenant of the apartments, a Christian brother in the fellowship, came downstairs. He asked me if everything was all right. I answered that it was. The man left and the ominous strangers introduced themselves to me as Galen Kelly and Graham Nance. They said the court order was probably just a misunderstanding and please hop in their car. I told them I had to go to work and drop off the readmission paperwork. They insisted everything would work out, to please get in the car. Well, I had a decision to make. I didn't like being told what to do. Should I make a run for it or oblige these men I didn't even know? I felt a real peace in me and even if I ran I was sure they were bent on taking me. I took another look and recognized my mother's signature on the paperwork. I felt a bit more at ease leaving with these guys in their car.

Normally, I would fear being kidnapped for ransom. My parents had wealth and a few people may want to exploit it. But I didn't sense urgency in these guys and believed it was really my mom who wished to initiate this type of meeting, whatever type of meeting it was to be. I wasn't taught to back down on issues and here was an opportunity to stand up. Of course, they didn't give me a clue what I needed to stand up for. My gut feeling was that it had something to do with my relationship with Jesus and impending marriage to Geri. I decided no matter what would happen I am strong in Jesus and He is strong in me. So I went in the car and we headed to see my parents in Chicago 150 miles away.

It was a quiet, uneventful three hour drive. Near O'Hare International Airport, we pulled up to the hotel. I was real curious about what was about to happen. We took the elevator to the ninth or tenth floor and as we got out, there stood my mom and step-dad in the hallway. Mom's first words were "I love you and we are doing this to help you" and gave me a big hug. I later found out, after my visit to Michigan with Geri earlier that year, mom was concerned with my mental health and spiritual well being due to my sudden life changes, decisions and actions. She was put in touch with Ben Martinez, a Phoenix, Arizona attorney. He procured a court order from a judge in DuPage County, Illinois to allow custodianship for my mom over me. All this was done to legally -at least in appearance- restrain me and have professional deprogrammers convince me my decisions were wrong to become a Christian and sever my connection with the No-Name Fellowship.

As we entered the hotel room there was several people there, but not my parents. Each person politely said hello, introduced themselves and Galen set the ground rules. He told me my parents love me, were concerned and invited this intervention into my life. There were body guards inside and outside my hotel room to protect me and keep me from leaving. Their goal was to do a lot of talking and point out the errors of my thought processes regarding religious beliefs. They had a saying, "We don't care if you worship doorknobs, as long as it is your own decision". I assured Galen I would not leave the room without his permission. I felt completely confident and at ease. If they want to talk, let's talk. I never felt physically threatened and I was ready for a challenge to test my beliefs.

Our schedule was pretty simple: for two hours each in the morning, afternoon and evening we would sit and talk, or rather, Galen, Graham and others would do the talking and I would listen. Galen, who was a deacon in his Episcopalian Church, was the team leader, Graham was an anti-terrorist expert and there were some former Moonies in the room. We stopped for meals or to watch sporting events on TV. I slept and ate well. I was not worn down by the process or deprived in any way, other than not being able to leave the room. I recall looking out my window overseeing the parking garage and noticed my car on the top deck. Wow, these guys move quickly. How did they do that? They must be really confident I'd move out of Urbana. All this just made me dig my heels in for a fight. I wanted to fight for my belief in the Messiah and to be with my friends and fiancée.

The two-hour discussions were about the bible, what Jews believe and why they don't believe in Jesus as the Messiah. This is where my training in the fellowship, studying the bible and discussions with the rabbi really helped. As it turns out, I knew the scriptures better than these guys. It really surprised me. I had no idea I knew as much as I did. I was not allowed to have a bible but thankfully, God's Spirit brought to my memory many verses and the strength to endure. All my personal study to become a believer in Jesus was brought to bear. I told these people that the bible is true, the prophecies of the coming Messiah are accurate and Jesus is the fulfillment of the Law who brought a new covenant through His life, death and resurrection from death.

When we were not "in session" the deprogrammers were some of the funniest people I ever met. Their sense of humor was clean and very dry. They made fun of world politics, historical references and even themselves. I played guitar, mostly Neil Diamond tunes, that not only endeared them, but also showed valuable proof that I was normal and had a mind for myself. Also, the deprogrammers were a bit surprised how up to date I was on the national news and sporting events. Their background was deprogramming young people from the Reverend Moon's Unification Church. I learned "Moonies" are completely cut off from the real world and have no interaction with family or friends. At this time, the No Name fellowship was nowhere near that type of mentality. It was a few years later that the extremes of the fellowship went too far.

During the second day at the hotel, I asked why the deprogrammers were so convinced my decision to become a believer was not of my own free will. They told me someone – a spy - was sent to infiltrate the group and gather information. I immediately knew who it was. The young man, Brad, came to a meeting early in the fall semester and stuck around for a few weeks and took off for home in Indiana.

Age 5 with a Princeton haircut.

Even then mom was thinking about the Ivy League for me.

Photo Courtesy of Goldberg Family Collection.

Bar Mitzvah at age 13.

Photo Courtesy of Goldberg Family Collection

Head Football Coach Bob Blackman on the sideline (ca 1975).

He was a fine gentleman and a very good coach.

Photo courtesy of University of Illinois Sports Information Office.

In uniform one last time (pictured with my children)
for the Alumni spring game against the Varsity (April 1987).

Photo Courtesy of Goldberg Family Collection.

At least that is the story he told us. He reported to my parents and Ben Martinez, the attorney, that the No Name Fellowship was a bunch of glassy-eyed zombies, blindly following the leaders, doing whatever the leaders said. Well, I don't know what Brad witnessed, but I'm sure he had some pre-conceived notions and couldn't differentiate a close community of believers from a closed off community. I will admit that we as a group and me personally were very dogmatic in our beliefs, even a bit defiant.

During one of the sessions, the deprogrammers began to verbally attack the leaders. Graham said the leaders of the fellowship had latent terrorist tendencies. I scoffed at that allegation.

The deprogrammers insisted the fellowship leaders were full of malice and had personal agendas to bolster their power. I know Pat Nipote doesn't have a hurtful bone in his body and Doug Keller doesn't use religion for financial purposes. Although Steve Schraeder, with all his talents, seemed a bit too salesmanship for me, I still had no reason or evidence to doubt his motives. All these people wanted to follow God and, although I concede they were a little young to lead a group of young Christians, I believe they didn't have it in them to purposefully deceive people for their own gain.

During another session, we discussed my personal life: the fact that I dropped out of school, my lack of communication with my family back home and my roommate. They accused me of being "lazy, money-grubbing, selfish, and homosexual". If I wasn't so mad at the accusation I would have laughed. What was this, time for good cop, bad cop? I dropped out of school, but was ready to return the next semester. I had no money and didn't ask for any from my parents. Lazy? I had plans to graduate from college and had my whole life ahead of me. Homosexual? My roommate was a captain on the football team who lived a much disciplined life of his own and I was engaged to be married! It was a crazy accusation. Nice try, guys.

The deprogrammers and I didn't celebrate Christmas, but we watched a lot of football on Christmas Day, which happened to be a Sunday. It didn't bother me not to celebrate Christmas because I know the Holy Spirit is with me every day. On the next Tuesday, Galen decided I was stable in my beliefs and thinking processes and we took off for Florida. The next phase was for me to be separate from the group for a period of time to make sure I made my own decisions particularly pertaining to my impending marriage.

Oh, my gosh, my fiancée!

I realized that Geri must be worried sick about me. I hadn't been able to contact anyone. Of course, in 1977, there was no wireless internet or cell phones. I later found out that dad contacted her and told her I just wanted to get away and think things over. On one hand, Geri was relieved to hear I was OK because she thought I might have been kidnapped for ransom. On the other hand, she knew me too well and didn't think it was my idea to leave town. She received support form her friends in Urbana while I was gone. Finally, when I arrived in Ft. Lauderdale, I was able to call Geri. It was funny, though, as we were driving around town from the airport to find Ben Martinez' Florida home, otherwise known as a "safe house," Galen got lost while driving the rental car. This was before GPS systems in cars. Since I had been to Miami and Ft Lauderdale several times vacationing with my parents, I knew the area. Ironically, I asked for the address and took them to the house.

Almost immediately, I called Geri. We were both relieved to hear each other's voices. We talked, prayed, laughed and cried. She asked me if I loved her and if we were going to be married. I said, "Yes and absolutely." In light of circumstances, we postponed our wedding date a second time, this time indefinitely and decided to talk about it later.

Geri told me so many people have been praying for me throughout Central Illinois and around the country. How did the word get out around the country? When Gene, the local Champaign Full Gospel Businessmen's leader, caught wind of my plight he asked for prayer for me through the Full Gospel Businessmen International network. Well, no wonder I felt confident and comfortable throughout the ordeal. People all over the world were praying for me and God answered!

After a couple days in Florida, the deprogrammers gave me freedom to roam around the city and relax. I took the time to walk along the seashore and read the bible.

My parents flew down and I visited with them. They looked worn out with worry. I reassured them everything was all right and I loved them.

By this time, one of my friends in Urbana contacted an attorney who became very concerned for my well-being. The attorney advised me to get out of Florida and come back to Urbana. I was, in his opinion, detained illegally. The court order was illegal and my rights were abused. Therefore, my family had no right to intervene and detain me. I took it under advisement. I must admit I was becoming homesick and wanted to return to Urbana. Galen was pressuring me to continue talks for my road to recovery. I told him, if my parents considered my "recovery" must include a renouncement of my beliefs, there would be no "recovery." There was a push from the deprogramming team in Florida for me to see the light and return to my original Jewish roots. Of course, I repeated that it is the most natural thing in the world for a Jew to become a follower of Jesus the Jewish Messiah.

I had enough. I contacted Geri's aunt in Fort Lauderdale, who gave me money for bus fare to Urbana and took off at dusk on Friday December 30. The bus drove through the night and arrived near Atlanta. As I stepped off to switch buses, I saw Kurt Martinez (son of Ben the attorney), one of the bodyguards from the deprogramming. I placed my wrists together as though he were going to handcuff me. He laughed and told me to relax. He was sent to make sure I was OK and ask if I would return to Fort Lauderdale. I asked him why. He said it would show a good faith effort to my parents that I could make my own decisions, talk to them one more time and bring closure to the situation. I relented and decided to return to Florida. I called Geri and she concurred with the decision. She felt uncomfortable with my leaving Fort Lauderdale in the first place.

Kurt drove us back to southern Florida and, upon our return, to my parents. Plans were made to fly Geri down. I hadn't seen Geri since December 22. That's more than a week; a long time for me not to see my girl! Once she arrived, we had a good time catching up and enjoyed the beautiful weather. She arrived on January 5th and stayed for four days. We went to the beach, visited with my parents and ate out a lot. It was like a vacation.

By this time, there was a young girl who was a Moonie staying at the safe house who was removed from her group in California. She was struggling with many issues, including being held against her will.

Geri and I talked to her from our perspective and shared bible verses with her comforting her with the love of God. We shared scripture on Jesus as the Savior and not to look to men for salvation and eternal guidance. The only intermediary between God and Man is Jesus; not Reverend Moon or any one else. We told her to search the scriptures and she will be set free. We prayed often with this fragile young lady. It was good for Geri and me to minister and feel used by God.

By the time Geri left for Urbana we mapped out a short-term plan. We continued the postponement of the wedding indefinitely and I would move to Michigan and try to finish my degree there. After all, what is a few months delay when you are going to spend a lifetime together? The purpose of my move to Michigan was one last effort to show my parents, who love me so much and pumped so much money into the deprogramming, that I was OK and could retain my beliefs regardless of geographic location.

VI.

THE FELLOWSHIP CHANGES

In mid-January, 1978, I moved to friend Kenny's house in Southfield, Michigan. I went to work for my dad selling steel. It was suggested I apply to Wayne State University so I could finish my business degree. It is an unusual move to transfer to another university with only 15 credit hours left to graduation. I happened to know the Dean of Students (I went top high school with her son) and due to my extraordinary circumstances she was able to have me admitted for the summer session.

After a few weeks I decided I wanted to be with my fiancée and friends in Urbana. I didn't enjoy working at my dad's office and I wanted to finish my degree at the University of Illinois. After all was said and done, I just wanted to go where I belonged. There was no one around in Detroit that I wanted to hang around. After prayer and discussion with Geri and others, I moved back to Urbana. Geri and I set a wedding date and we were married on Saturday, March 18, 1978. After postponing for several months we were ready to celebrate. Although not excited about the event, my parents attended the wedding and I was very happy to see them.

Geri and I were married at a church with a small reception at the fellowship hall in the same building. Although not the first mixed marriage in our family, I'm sure it was a little unsettling for my parents to attend a Christian ceremony at a church for their Jewish born and raised son. The ceremony was basic with vows and rings and a short homily by the minister from the church, who presided over the nuptials. Several of the fellowship leaders came forward to pray a blessing over Geri and me, what we called "laying on of hands in prayer." I'm sure this exacerbated the idea my folks thought I was still involved in a religious cult.

Some of our Christian friends decorated the reception hall and set up the dessert buffet beforehand. We took some wedding pictures after the ceremony and by time we entered the reception, most of the appetizers and desserts were gone. There were many congratulations and I was happy to finally marry my wife.

We drove a couple hours to a hotel in the western Chicago suburbs and celebrated our wedding night. The next day we flew to Orlando, Florida for our honeymoon. We had a great time seeing all the sights and enjoying all the benefits of being married. Nine months to the day after our wedding night, our son, Jacob David, was born.

Jacob was named, in part, after my Grandpa Dave who treated my family so well while growing up in Oak Park, Michigan. By the time I was 10 years old, he suffered a stroke. Before he died, he could mutter only three Hebrew words, "elohey velohey visholem" which from the Hebrew means "God is a God of Peace." Geri convinced me to invite my father, Moris, to meet our new born son. I hadn't seen Moris in several years but it was a good reunion. I found out that Grandpa's full name was David Jacob.

Over the next couple of years, there were many changes in philosophy and activity in the fellowship. We met on Sunday mornings and moved our services from various places on or near campus: from Christian Campus House, Armory House, the New Life Church building, and finally the Jefferson Building in Champaign. Each meeting we generally had a bible study, with singing of praise and worship songs and some open sharing from group members. Usually, Doug or Steve would finish the meetings with a mini-sermon on some topic dealing with walking daily with Jesus in a stronger commitment. By 1979, there was a tight band of followers of Doug's teachings gleaned from Doug's many trips and meetings with itinerant preachers.

There were guests and visitors who came by from time to time to share their version of the gospel and a better walk with Jesus. Derek passed through from England and talked about the authority of God, the leadership of men and introduced head coverings for the women to wear. Mel Colbert came over from Ireland and eventually lived full time in Urbana. He tutored Doug on the scriptures and leading a religious flock. Stacy was a prophet and preacher from California who came to stir the pot to move people to grow closer to God. Each of these men had a spiritual, prophetic gift to speak directly into people lives. The purpose of prophecy is to encourage people to grow closer to God, but in hindsight, the result was more destructive than helpful to the people in the fellowship.

In the book of Corinthians, much is written on the gifts of the Holy Spirit and the equipping of believers with those gifts. There is also the five-fold ministry: apostle, prophet, evangelist, teacher, and preacher. The leaders in the fellowship believed these offices are to be filled today. As Derek, Mel, and Stacy came through town they would fuel these teachings. As they did, prophecies over individuals began to increase. First, there were general words from the Lord, such as "God will meet your needs", or "Jesus has blessed you abundantly". Later, there were some specific instructions given through prophesy. "Your parents will be strong against your faith" and "Educate yourself in the Lord, not of men". These instructions were interpreted to separate oneself from family and grow closer to the fellowship community. We felt it was part of the persecution we were to receive for righteousness sake, when in reality it became a self-fulfilling prophecy. By sharing a gospel of hell, fire and brimstone we placed ourselves above others and didn't allow God through His Holy Spirit of love and grace to work in us.

One of the elements the leaders tried to incorporate was community life as described in the first and second chapter of the Book of Acts in the New Testament. The leaders came to believe and taught that the fellowship group was a corporate Christian body and stuck with each other through thick and thin, much as a family would. They taught persecution from family members and others would increase as each person's commitment to Jesus increased. According to the gospel of the fellowship you cannot be close to your blood family and be committed to the family of God. This is quite the opposite of what Jesus preached regarding community.

That is not to say we didn't have fun. We had a "Brothers" softball team and flag football team in the Champaign Park District. We lined up Illinois varsity letter-winners like no other team in the area: five Illinois letter-winners and two more who participated on the varsity level were on our softball team. For example, we rarely had a single. There was so much speed that we usually stretched the hit into a double. We had speed, power, strength and talent. We rarely lost and had fun playing.

The fellowship group served well as an unofficial halfway house for drug addicts and homeless people. We would take people in our homes and after hearing the gospel message and accepting the power of God's love those new souls in Christ would clean up their lives and become productive members of the community.

Also during this period of time, several people in the fellowship, particularly the women, were discovering a bad trend in the group. God bless the women. My own wife could not grasp the direction of inwardness and guilt manipulation that was laden by the leaders. Her testimony in Jesus betrays the other gospel ("repent or perish") taught by the fellowship leaders at that time. If anyone has felt the emotional healing, love and grace of Jesus, it is Geri. After several emotional issues as a teenager and failed marriage at a young age, she came to the knowledge of God's salvation message with His saving grace and forgiveness. Geri could be the poster woman for God. She hit the bottom of life's experiences and despair and Jesus showed her the way to eternal life, forgiveness and a new life as a Christian.

In many ways, the fellowship became a closed community. We lived in small groups in various apartment complexes in Champaign-Urbana. Instead of showing love to all people, we would only love those who accepted our gospel and would disengage ourselves from others. The elders made a push to come against other religions, particularly the Catholics. There was an almost national movement by Christian evangelicals to knock the Catholics and our group jumped on the bandwagon. We felt there were too much liturgy and not enough freedom to follow Jesus and have an individual relationship with Him. What we didn't notice is that we were becoming the very thing we were preaching against. We became caught up in the law of doing good deeds and avoiding bad and not learning about an individual relationship with Jesus. We would teach it, but not BE it. Originally, being humble before God was part of our life; now we placed ourselves above others as a more perfect church group.

During the fall of 1980, there were at least three highly-involved families that decided to leave the fellowship based on problems in the leadership. This caused quite a ruckus in the group and the leadership decided to "shun" these families. The followers were instructed to leave the families alone and not have contact with them.

In a related issue, later that year, Doug and Steve were contemplating leaving the fellowship. The reasons weren't made clear publicly, but the very idea of leaving shook the faithful few; by now numbering about 125 people. In January 1981, a deal was struck in the leadership with Pat Nipote and Steve Schraeder to step down as elders.

Coming to light at this time was Steve's public confession that he lied when he shared previously his testimony on so many public occasions. When he told his story, Steve had a very dynamic time coming to the gospel of Jesus. He told his testimony in great fashion, but now confessed to some inaccuracies. Due to his lies, he was made an example and stepped down from leadership. But Steve was not alone in his public confessions. It was expected, if a person made a gross error of judgment they would get in front of the congregation and confess the sin. I never did it, but others thought it was a cleansing time in their life. I believe in confessing sins to the Father in Heaven with Jesus as our mediator and with Him as the propitiation for sin I can receive immediate forgiveness. Confessions in front of a group seemed wrong to me. The philosophy in the group was if you sinned to God (the Head of the Church) you also sinned to the body (group members). Part of the hypocrisy in the group was when people confessed sin, they were looked down upon. When Doug confessed sin, it was as though he carried a badge of honor.

By the end of February 1981, Pat Nipote left the fellowship. This left Doug Keller as the sole elder in the Fellowship. He appointed his brother Denny, Jim McDonnell and Don Elliott as elders. Many members of the group, including myself, became disillusioned by these events. I was especially put off that young men who were not married and had no children were named elders and asked to be leaders. Many in the group were upset that the Nipotes who helped found the group, left without public explanation. When I talked personally with Patrick, he told me that he tried his best to keep the group on the right path, particularly trying to get it hooked up with an established evangelical church, but Doug would have no part in it. By this time, I had private thoughts that Doug was striving for power and to have total control of the group, but until Pat's admission I had no corroboration.

I decided to leave the fellowship. I could not be part of changes that seemed to be leading the group down a destructive road. When I went to Doug's apartment to tell him of my decision he assured me that the new leadership would walk and talk in a manner worthy of following God and they would not lead the sheep astray. Doug told me they were receiving much counsel from other respected people outside the fellowship. I wasn't totally convinced, but decided to give Doug and the new leaders a chance to prove themselves.

In the spring of 1981, the New Jersey fellowship (a satellite group) flourished as a result of Doug's frequent trips back to his hometown. Also, Spokane had a small fellowship group affiliated to our group as a result of one of Doug's trips and speaking engagements. He challenged people to follow God and not men. As a result, a thriving church split with about 50 people to form the new Spokane fellowship group.

A couple months later, in May 1981, I decided again to leave the group. I wasn't happy and didn't feel the joy of Jesus in my life. I recall sitting in Denny Keller's living room and he related a dream of falling terra cotta roof shingles from a house. He felt I was like a lost shingle and the rains would come in my home and destroy it. The interpretation Denny gave was that if I left the fellowship, I would be shunned and lose favor in God. Instead of high-tailing it and running, I believed him. I was guilt-manipulated into staying in the group. I decided to get more involved by leading prayers, singing solos and putting together some bible teachings for Sunday services. Some people were looking to me for guidance and I started to feel better about myself. In spite of the manipulation, my faith in Jesus grew, which was important since I was facing other issues in my life.

Over the following three years, I was promoted several times in a local restaurant chain. I became an assistant store manager, store manager and, finally, at age 24, an assistant general manager in the central office. My responsibilities included purchasing for the central warehouse, payroll, liaison between the store managers and central office and helping with store expansion. During summer 1981, interest rates shot up and it became difficult for the corporation to open new stores. This cut my work time in half and the owner decided to cut expansion and offered me an opportunity to manage a store until the company starting expanding again. I thought and prayed about it. I didn't feel comfortable going back into a store management position. I applied at different businesses and interviewed on the UI campus for a position as the assistant director position food services. I told the elders about it and when it came to light I would work some Sundays they told me to decline the offer. I was caught between having a good job or obeying the council of the elders and losing esteem in the leaders. I decided not to take the job offer. Although I was out of work, the decision seemed to elevate me in the eyes of the leadership. The way the fellowship operated, apparently if you turned down prosperity and had a more difficult road to hoe, then Jesus seemed to intervene more in your spiritual walk. For the next several months, I knocked around town doing odd jobs, supporting my wife and two small children (our second child, Leah, was born in the summer 1980).

At one point, we were so broke that we barely had enough food in the cupboards to feed the children. Geri and I prayed and a small miracle happened. There was a bag of groceries with a giant homemade loaf of bread. It was like manna from heaven, just like when God fed the Hebrews in the desert after their release from bondage from the Egyptians. We started to rely on God for our daily provisions. Geri, as was the custom in the fellowship, was a stay at home mom.

One of the idiosyncrasies we picked up was each family decided to get rid of our televisions. We felt there was too much "worldliness" that compromised our walk with Jesus. It became part of fellowship meeting testimonies how we would take the TV to the dumpster and smash it so no one else could use it.

March 1982 was another turning point for the fellowship. Sue Pathos, who was engaged to marry a young man in our group, was kidnapped. Word got back to us that her parents had taken her to prevent the marriage and get her out of the fellowship. The fiancé was crushed. He made contact with her to confirm she was all right and he learned the stories about kidnapping and deprogramming were true. Soon, other members of the group were taken against their will. Many people left the group. The word "cult" kept cropping up. Parents in Chicago area were furious with the changes in the lives of their children and decided to make some changes themselves. They became aggressive and hired a professional deprogrammer. The ringleader for the parents was Vic Jones, a resident of Park Ridge, Illinois who was a labor - management arbitrator. I knew Vic from the early days in the fellowship when I worked part time in a gas/service station in Champaign and he'd come down to visit his son Dan, who also worked there. Vic was a very intense guy; a true type-A personality. He could take on several tasks simultaneously, get the job done and do it well. He was a chain-smoker and had health problems. He always seemed a bit nervous to me, in the sense of getting ulcers, but he loved his family. He had a big heart and when the Chicago parents included him in the kidnappings, he basically took over, got it organized and hired the best people available. There was a lot of money that exchanged hands particularly for the benefit of the deprogrammers.

Many parents had lost contact with their children. The elders taught cutting yourself from your family was the biblical thing to do. The leaders twisted the scripture where Jesus talks about families being at odds with one another because of the gospel (see Matthew chapter 10). However, the elders forced the issue and instead of sharing Good News with love and grace we caused a separation of intolerance for others. The brethren in the fellowship replaced our family. During this time over several months, there was a step up in legalism. Along with women wearing head coverings, everyone dressed plainly, with no adornment, and elders were more involved in everyday decisions for people. Eating habits were scrutinized and professional medical help, although not stopped completely, was to be covered by prayer and God's direct intervention.

Personally, I needed a change of scenery. Geri and I prayed about it and wanted to move to Spokane, Washington. With everything going on in Illinois, I thought we could be of service to the Christian brothers and sisters out west and be a calming influence to them. I didn't have a job to keep me in the Midwest and it seemed a good time for a move. The elders concurred, particularly when Mel Colbert, the Irishman now living in Spokane, said he felt God wanted me out there too. Receiving a blessing from such an important man made me feel special in the group. So we moved.

Going west was quite an adventure. We sold our home, packed all our belongings in a 24-foot moving van and hitched our 1972 Chevy Carryall to it. We put our plants and nick-knacks in the Chevy. Six weeks earlier (April 1982) Geri gave birth to our second daughter, Hannah. We took two other people with our family. Diane Smith was set to marry Rush Green in Spokane and we took Mona, a 22-year old single girl. I drove the van while the women traded off driving the station wagon loaded up with with the kids. This was my first cross-country driving trip to the west with family. One night, we stayed in a small motel in Montana which had an oil-burning furnace that no one knew how to operate. Several of us slept on the floor and it was a good thing the temperature did not drop under 40 degrees. Our body heat kept the room warm enough. After all, it was June, but the mountain air was cool at night.

The next day we decided to venture up Mount Rushmore. We had four adults and three children and decided to take both vehicles. We kept the Chevy hitched and took the van up the mountain with the station wagon leading the way. Well, that didn't last long as the steep grades caused us to turn around. We got to Spokane the next day without ever seeing any of the stone presidents.

The balance of summer 1982 was relatively uneventful in Spokane. I changed jobs from selling copier machines to managing a gas station/car wash combination business. It appeared the deprogrammings in Champaign had ceased. About 30 people were kidnapped in Illinois and almost 80 people left the fellowship throughout the three cities. However, in late August, Dan and Jeannette Jones (Vic Jones' son) who lived in Spokane went missing. Of course, we should have known. Vic had them kidnapped (or as he called it, "intervened") and deprogrammed from the group. A few days later, Dan showed up at my door and said they were moving to Illinois and leaving the fellowship. Dan didn't want to leave without saying goodbye. He seemed very tired, but certain in his decision. He invited me to see him off at the airport the next day.

At the airport I greeted Dan and Jeannette and Vic Jones was there. Vic came to me and held tight onto my arm. He strongly urged me to fly back with him to Chicago. I politely refused and said I had a job and family in Spokane. He said not to worry; all the arrangements could be made in very short order to take care of all my needs. I thanked him and said "no".

There were some wonderful families Geri and I knew in Spokane. Gary and Nancy Grosse were very strong followers of Jesus and had several children in a very large house. Nancy became known as a "mother of Israel" in the sense of having so much experience that all the women wanted her advice. The Nelsons had two young sons and a beautiful home in a wealthy neighborhood. Geri and I, with our three children lived on Kiernan Street across the way from Dave and Georgia Krane. Dave had been a successful business man but had a nervous breakdown a couple years previous to our arrival.

My relationship with my mom and dad became strained. I rarely called them and I knew they were unhappy with my lifestyle of living in Spokane and making a small amount of money at what they considered a dead end job as a gas station manager.

On Saturdays, many members of the fellowship would go to Riverfront Park (where the World's Fair was held in 1974) and do public preaching. We wouldn't talk to anyone in particular, just who-ever would stop and listen. We picked up this habit from our days preaching on the Quad at Illinois during the lunch hour after two itinerant preachers, Jed and Max, showed us how. One fine morning, I took a turn at speaking aloud to a small crowd and one heckler turned on the sprinkling system. I was soaking wet. However, it wasn't all bad as it was 90 degrees and the water cooled me off.

Sunday morning worship services were very long. We started at 9 a.m. and sometimes not finish until 1 p.m. There wasn't a nursery or Sunday school for kids, so they just sat there, usually squirming, until the end of the meeting. They became hungry and cranky. In fact, if a member's child did not react poorly, they were deemed an ideal parent with children under control of God's spirit. It was thought your children are being fed by the Spirit of God, so food can wait even in long meetings. Geri and I had a problem with this twisted philosophy. Worship on the other hand was very good. We had a guitarist who led some wonderful songs we could sing to exalt the name and life of Jesus. Personal prophesies abounded. There were usually five or six of them in each service. Most of them were phrases like "God the Father wants to bless you immensely" or "Be still and know I am God". Usually pretty harmless and verses straight from the bible. They were meant to be words of encouragement from one person to another. However, every now and then, a word came forth that was more corrective in nature. "Walk in the way of the Lord and stay away from the foolishness of your earthly family." These types of phrases and so called prophecies were meant to draw a division between the person and their family back home. Even with the kidnappings and deprogrammings, Doug Keller made sure the fellowship stayed on course to follow his so-called "counsel of God" and his authority placed on earth. Simply, as Doug taught it, we were facing the persecution of men because of our faith in Christ. The apostles of the first century faced it, even to death, and therefore we faced persecution as well. It became a vicious cycle, a self-fulfilling prophecy, the more defiant to a normal way of life we were, the more the parents got upset with us and vice versa.

Doug Keller was the resident elder in Spokane and in the fall of 1982 several elders from Urbana, Illinois came to visit him. The men from Illinois told Doug they had seen the light and that the group was on the wrong track. Love and grace were missing within the fellowship. There was too much "holier than thou" business. Don Elliott, visiting from Urbana, was in my living room recounting this to me. Don was a friend of mine since his days as a student manager on the football team. He is a man of great integrity and tears came to my eyes as the revelation of love and leadership came into focus in his life. Unfortunately, although Keller listened, he did not harken to good advice from the Urbana elders. In fact, Keller twisted all the words back to the men and they went back home with their tails between their legs and repented for their wrongdoing of trying to correct him.

A few short months later, Mel Colbert, the Irishmen who also was a resident elder in Spokane, contracted cancer and was terminally ill. On his death bed, Mel told Doug that everything they had been teaching about authority and elders leading peoples' lives was wrong. Mel said that God is in each person and that relationship should prevail. Elders were merely administrators of the church and available for counsel, not instigators to direct peoples' lives. Charles Kroll, one of the older men who occasionally came to preach to us, was at Mel's bedside and later told me the story. I asked him about Doug's reaction. Kroll said Doug rejected Mel's death bed confession and said Mel was wrong.

This was heavy duty stuff for me. I thought my coming to Spokane would be a stabilizing influence for the group and yet, with Doug's arrival, a harsher gospel came forth.

VII.

EXPECT THE UNEXPECTED

In July 1983, my parents asked me to come to Detroit with my family for a vacation. We hadn't been there in almost two years and it would be good for my folks to see the grandkids. It's been almost a year since the last kidnapping and deprogramming and I joked with Geri maybe we would be next. We made plans to go and Geri asked a Christian sister in the fellowship to borrow a swimsuit. She refused and Geri thought it odd. The Christian sister said she didn't feel comfortable loaning the suit for the cousins club meeting in Detroit because she felt Geri shouldn't go.

We arrived in Detroit on Friday, July 22nd. That Sunday, a brunch was scheduled at Linda Harris' house, a friend of my sister, Ruth. Our kids were with my other sister, Sheryl, and excited about going to the beach and hanging out with Vivian, Sheryl's dog. Geri and I entered Linda's house and there was a wonderful spread of food; bagels, lox, cream cheese, tomatoes with coffee and juices.

Other than noticing some unfamiliar people, it was a typical Sunday morning feast in a Jewish home.

My mom called Geri and me into to one of the bedrooms. She said she loved us dearly and wanted to have some people talk to us. Geri and I looked at each other and rolled our eyes. NOT AGAIN! If it wasn't so serious we would have started laughing. All kinds of people entered into the house. We were set up! A couple of the young men we knew from Urbana, Illinois arrived. Bob and Marty, otherwise known as the original "dorm zealots," in the fellowship were there to make sure we wouldn't escape and offer information and advice as needed. A former Moonie walked in and explained the rules. She said they were not going to hold us against our will, but wanted to explain a few things. Weren't we curious as to why so many people left the fellowship a year ago? My mom wanted to give us an opportunity to leave the group on our own terms. Thus, the family intervention to rescue our minds from a cult began.

A day later Dave Clark showed up. He is a professional deprogrammer (interventionist) who was once in a cult. He told us he is a Baptist and his interest is not to disturb our Christian faith, but to show us how the fellowship is a cult and why we should leave the group as soon as possible. Of course, there was a certain trust factor missing. How could I trust someone who was so against my friends, elders and therefore, I concluded, against the Gospel? Nevertheless, we decided to stay and listen.

We viewed several videos including movies on Jim Jones and the Peoples Temple suicide cult in Jonestown, Guyana. That was a scary story; how one man could control the destiny and deaths of over 900 people. We watched a made for TV movie called "The Wave" starring Bruce Davison. Here is a synopsis from Wikipedia:

"To explain to his students the atmosphere in the 1930's Nazi-Germany, history teacher Burt Ross initiates a daring experiment. He declares himself leader of a new movement, called "The Wave." Inspired, he proclaims ideas about Power, Discipline and Superiority. His students are strikingly willing to follow him. Soon the entire school is under the spell of "The Wave." Anyone who refuses to be a part of the Movement faces threats or worse. Ross himself gets carried away by his own experiment. Or has it turned into something more than an experiment? A climax is unavoidable, resulting in a hard lesson for both Ross and his students... *Written by Diederik B.A. Rep"*

One of the lessons learned is how easily people can give up their independence and free will to follow another person. While viewing the movie I quickly caught on to the concept.

Dave Clark taught Geri and me the elements of what constitutes a cult (religious or otherwise) or ideological totalism. Most of the concepts come from a book, "Thought Reform and the Psychology of Totalism", written by Robert Jay Lifton, (1963, pp419ff). Below is an edited excerpt taken from a summary of the chapter (see citation at the end of this chapter). Lifton, a psychiatrist and distinguished professor at the City University of New York, has studied the psychology of extremism for decades. He testified at the 1976 bank robbery trial of Patty Hearst about the theory of "coercive persuasion."

Milieu Control – The control of information and communication. The most basic feature of the thought reform environment, the psychological current upon which all else depends, is the control of human communication. Through this milieu control the totalist environment seeks to establish domain over not only the individual's communication with the outside (all that he sees and hears, reads or writes, experiences, and expresses), but also - in its penetration of his inner life - over what we may speak of as his communication with himself. Thought reform participants may be in doubt as to who is telling what to whom, but the fact that extensive information about everyone is being conveyed to the authorities is always known.

Mystical Manipulation – The manipulation of experiences that appear spontaneous but in fact were planned and orchestrated. The inevitable next step after milieu control is extensive personal manipulation. This manipulation assumes a no-holds-barred character, and uses every possible device at the milieu's command, no matter how bizarre or painful. Initiated from above, it seeks to provoke specific patterns of behavior and emotion in such a way that these will appear to have arisen spontaneously, directed as it is by an ostensibly omniscient group, must assume, for the manipulated, a near-mystical quality. At the level of the individual person, the psychological responses to this manipulative approach revolve about the basic polarity of trust and mistrust. One is asked to accept these manipulations on a basis of ultimate trust (or faith): "like a child in the arms of its mother." He who trusts in this degree can experience the manipulations within the idiom of the mystique behind them: that is, he may welcome their mysteriousness, find pleasure in their pain, and feel them to be necessary for the fulfillment of the "higher purpose" which he endorses as his own. But such elemental trust is difficult to maintain; and even the strongest can be dissipated by constant manipulation.

Demand for Purity – In the thought reform milieu, as in all situations of ideological totalism, the experiential world is sharply divided into the pure and the impure, into the absolutely good and the absolutely evil. The good and the pure are of course those ideas, feelings, and actions which are consistent with the totalist ideology and policy; anything else is apt to be relegated to the bad and the impure. Nothing human is immune from the flood of stern moral judgments. All "taints" and "poisons" which contribute to the existing state of impurity must be searched out and eliminated. At the level of the relationship between individual and environment, the demand for purity creates what we may term a *guilty milieu* and a *shaming milieu*. Since each man's impurities are deemed sinful

113

and potentially harmful to himself and to others, he is, so to speak, expected to expect punishment - which results in a relationship of guilt and his environment. Similarly, when he fails to meet the prevailing standards in casting out such impurities, he is expected to expect humiliation and ostracism - thus establishing a relationship of shame with his milieu. Moreover, the sense of guilt and the sense of shame become highly-valued: they are preferred forms of communication, objects of public competition, and the basis for eventual bonds between the individual and his totalist accusers. One may attempt to simulate them for a while, but the subterfuge is likely to be detected, and it is safer to experience them genuinely.

Confession – Sins, as defined by the group, are to be confessed either to a personal monitor or publicly to the group. There is the demand that one confess to crimes one has not committed, to sinfulness that is artificially induced, in the name of a cure that is arbitrarily imposed. Such demands are made possible not only by the ubiquitous human tendencies toward guilt and shame but also by the need to give expression to these tendencies. In totalist hands, confession becomes a means of exploiting, rather than offering solace for, these vulnerabilities. Also, the more I accuse myself, the more I have a right to judge others.

Sacred Science – The group's doctrine or ideology is considered to be the ultimate Truth, beyond all questioning or dispute. The assumption here is not so much that man can be God, but rather that man's *ideas* can be God. A follower is prevented from engaging in the receptive search for truth which characterizes the genuinely scientific approach. The sacred science represents another continuous pressure toward personal closure, toward avoiding, rather than grappling with, the kinds of knowledge and experience necessary for genuine self-expression and for creative development.

Loading the Language – The group interprets or uses words and phrases in new ways so that often the outside world does not understand. The language of the totalist environment is characterized by the thought-terminating cliché. The most far-reaching and complex of human problems are compressed into brief, highly reductive, definitive-sounding phrases, easily memorized and easily expressed. To be sure, this kind of language exists to some degree within any cultural or organizational group, and all systems of belief depend upon it. It is in part an expression of unity and exclusiveness: as Edward Sapir put it, "'He talks like us' is equivalent to saying 'He is one of us.'" The loading is much more extreme in ideological totalism, however, since the jargon expresses the claimed certitudes of the sacred science. For an individual person, the effect of the language of ideological totalism can be summed up in one word: constriction. He is, so to speak, linguistically deprived; and since language is so central to all human experience, his capacities for thinking and feeling are immensely narrowed. This is what Hu

meant when he said, "using the same pattern of words for so long...
you feel chained." Actually, not everyone exposed *feels* chained, but
in effect everyone *is* profoundly confined by these verbal fetters. As
in other aspects of totalism, this loading may provide an initial sense
of insight and security, eventually followed by uneasiness. This
uneasiness may result in a retreat into a rigid orthodoxy in which
an individual shouts the ideological jargon all the louder in order to
demonstrate his conformity, hide his own dilemma and his despair,
and protect himself from the fear and guilt he would feel should he
attempt to use words and phrases other than the correct ones. Or
else he may adapt a complex pattern of inner division, and duti-
fully produce the expected cliché's in public performances while in
his private moments he searches for more meaningful avenues of
expression. Either way, his imagination becomes increasingly dis-
sociated from his actual life experiences and may tend to atrophy
from disuse.

Doctrine over person – The member's personal experiences
are subordinated to the sacred science and any contrary experiences
must be denied or reinterpreted to fit the ideology of the group.
This sterile language reflects characteristic feature of ideological
totalism: the subordination of human experience to the claims of
doctrine. This primacy of doctrine over person is evident in the
continual shift between experience itself and the highly abstract
interpretation of such experience - between genuine feelings and

spurious cataloguing of feelings. It has much to do with the peculiar aura of half-reality which totalist environment seems, at least to the outsider, to possess. The underlying assumption is that the doctrine - including its mythological elements - is ultimately more valid, true, and real than is any aspect of actual human character or human experience. Thus, even when circumstances require that a totalist movement follow a course of action in conflict with or outside of the doctrine. The individual person who finds himself under such doctrine-dominated pressure to change is thrust into an intense struggle with his own sense of integrity, a struggle which takes place in relation to polarized feelings of sincerity and insincerity.

Dispensing of existence – The group has the prerogative to decide who has the right to exist and who does not. The totalist environment draws a sharp line between those whose right to existence can be recognized, and those who possess no such right. Are not men presumptuous to appoint themselves the dispensers of human existence? Surely this is a flagrant expression of what the Greeks called *hubris*, of arrogant man making himself God. Yet one underlying assumption makes this arrogance mandatory: the conviction that there is just one path to true existence, just one valid mode of being, and that all others are perforce invalid and false. Totalists thus feel themselves compelled to destroy all possibilities of false existence as a means of furthering the great plan of true existence to which they are committed.

Why are people drawn into totalist population? The degree of individual totalism involved depends greatly upon factors in one's personal history: early lack of trust, extreme environmental chaos, total domination by a parent or parent-representative, intolerable burdens of guilt, and severe crises of identity. Thus an early sense of confusion and dislocation, or an early experience of unusually intense family milieu control, can produce later a complete intolerance for confusion and dislocation, and a longing for the reinstatement of milieu control. But these things are in some measure part of every childhood experience; and therefore the potential for totalism is a continuum from which no one entirely escapes, and in relationship to which no two people are exactly the same.

Citation: The Ross Institute Internet Archives for the Study of Destructive Cults, Controversial Groups and Movements. They are taken from Chapter 22 of Robert Jay Lifton's book," Thought Reform and the Psychology of Totalism: A Study of 'Brainwashing' in China." First published in 1961, his book was reprinted in 1989 by the University of North Carolina Press.

VIII.

BORN AGAIN, AGAIN

As Geri and I waded through the information, we had to distinguish what was truly God-centered in the group and what was being manipulated by the leaders. We didn't believe the elders acted for their own material gain or simply to control, but deceived themselves into believing that what they were doing was right. Regardless, we owed it to ourselves and our well-being, as well as our children, to evaluate everything that was said in these meetings. Since we were "strongly requested" not to leave the house, we decided to make the most of a difficult situation. It appeared to us that involvement in the fellowship contained at least a little bit of each element of totalism. However, Geri and I fought off most verbal attacks on the leaders in the fellowship from the deprogrammers because we believed the leaders' motives were pure. Once we were able to separate motives from actions and consequences we were able to see more clearly the fallibilities of the leadership. Instead of defending their motives we took a deeper look at the behaviors and actions of the elders. We were able to see clearly how destructive their messages became in the lives of the followers.

Throughout the process of teaching us about totalism and leaders' behaviors, the deprogrammers talked about how common sense, logic and reasoning should be used to make sound judgments. So many decisions were made for us; we almost didn't know how to make a decision on our own. This is not to say I wasn't liable for my actions. After each directive from the leadership I made a decision whether to follow it or not.

I quickly point out that Scripture is a very large influence in decision making and life decisions. How could one argue with the wisdom of the Book of Proverbs or the spiritual depth of Psalms? Geri and I prayed every day for God to give us strength and understanding throughout the ordeal. We clung to His promise that He would never leave nor forsake us. His Holy Spirit felt very much alive in us; giving us courage to stand in the wake of difficult decisions.

Dave Clark and his helpers were an enormous encouragement to us. They affirmed our Christian beliefs while describing the bad behaviors and directives of the group leaders. The information and evidence was piling up. After a few days we were getting tired of the discussions and debates and missing our children immensely.

We finally snapped. After six days the proverbial light bulb went off in our heads and the decision dawned on us: we can and we will remove ourselves from the fellowship; it would be a great detriment to us and our children to stay in the group. Although enlightened and relieved, we were exhausted. Although not deprived of food or sleep, it was difficult to rest at night with the entire information gathering and the weight of an impending life decision. David Clark was true to his word. He gave us the important information for us to leave the group and keep our faith in Jesus Christ intact. Although we didn't know where we would attend church, we knew we were part of the Church. Jesus never let go of us and we certainly hung to him for dear eternal life. Though tired physically and emotionally we felt good about our decisions.

Before Dave left, he gave us contact information for following up for life after a cult. There is a place called "Unbound" in Iowa City, The Cult Awareness Network (CAN) and individuals who left the fellowship and similar groups who have an understanding of authoritarianism to serve as resources.

So, why was it necessary to go through a deprogramming or as it is called nowadays, exit counseling? It basically gave us knowledge and the courage to follow through with what we couldn't do on our own. Finally, we relied upon the Holy Spirit, common sense and our own best interests to leave the group. Once and for all time, we knew we couldn't be guilt manipulated into staying with the group as happened twice before.

After leaving the group, Geri and I are periodically asked what to look for in a possible authoritative group. I try to give them a list in laymen terms. Following is some information of how a person may recognize cult activities. To be fair, I am aware there are some legitimate churches and groups that may fit some of the elements of a totalist group. We need to beware of an anti-cult cult mentality. Be careful; these are guidelines, not rules.

Oftentimes, destructive cults arise on college campuses. This is a prime environment for leaders to prey on young people separated from the warmth and security of a loving home.

Here are some indicators for parents to look for:

– Sudden changes in personality. For example shy vs. outgoing, sense of humor, lack of interest in hobbies such as music, sports, etc.

– Removing oneself from relationships with family and friends and spending more time within the group. Moving towards total involvement with the group to the exclusion of others.

– Highly motivated to share group's ideologies and do fund-raising to support leaders possibly to the exclusion of financial well being of the student.

– Phrases and word usage becomes synonymous with the group think and doctrine.

Signs for students to look for:

– Authoritative and charismatic leader of the group.

– Heavy push to a high level of group conformity without respect to your individualism.

– Love bombing. Group shows love and support as you accept their beliefs.

– Must sever relationships to family, friends and other religions.

– Opportunities to isolate you from your regular environments.

Finally, the best axiom I can say is, "If it feels wrong, it probably is and get out."

Our ordeal in Southfield, Michigan lasted 10 days. Geri and I agreed to go to "Unbound" in Iowa. Their mission is to provide exit counseling and teaching tools for reintegration into society. It was very important to my parents that we go through the process. Geri and I felt we already had what we needed to get on with our lives. Out of love and respect for my parents, we decided to go.

We spent six long days there. We missed our children and there was nothing important to do but read books. We watched some TV, particularly movies. We hadn't done that in a long time. At least the staff had a sense of humor; there was a one panel cartoon on a wall that read "Frisbyterians – people who worship Frisbees stuck on a roof" with a picture illustrating the sentiment.

On August 7th, we arrived at my parents' house and held our children tight for several minutes. They had a great time at my sister's place and playing in the lake by her house. I really appreciate how my family sacrificed their time and made great efforts to look after our children while we were gone for two weeks. Our kids were fine. Geri and I missed them immensely.

We decided to take my parents' offer and live with them for a month or two while we shopped for a home in the Detroit northwest suburban area. After a few days, I flew to Spokane, loaded up a rental van of all our belongings and moved everything cross country to Farmington Hills, Michigan. I began job hunting and while looking for a job I really wanted, I worked for Wendy's International as a store manager. A couple months later I landed a job as a financial services rep for a floorplanning company. Floorplanning is when a company pays the invoices for a retailer and the retailer pays the floorplanner back with interest when items are sold.

As part of our early reintegration into society in Michigan, Geri and I took stock of our Christian beliefs. We wanted to separate what we believe from what other people made us believe. An easy adaptation to make in our minds is how authority operated in the fellowship (very demeaning and demanding) to a more genteel approach (prayerful and supportive). The general tenets of faith are left intact. I became most interested in bottom line faith, such as:

–The Bible is inspired by God and therefore is the Holy Scriptures.

– There is only one true and living God.

– Man is God's creation and willingly falls into sin.

– Jesus is God's Son and is both divine and human.

– Jesus, the Jewish Messiah, died for the sins of all mankind and rose from the dead and all who believe have eternal life with Him.

There are other doctrines that would become cornerstones of our beliefs over the next several months, but these were the most important. We didn't realize what wonderful blessings would come our way in very short order during our search for truth.

I became reacquainted with my family, high school friends, coaches and teachers. They were all interested in my faith and ordeals I faced over the past few years. Although willing to share my testimony as to how I became a Christian, it was difficult to tell others of my brainwashing in a religious movement. How could an intelligent, educated man such as me fall prey to such an environment? The best answer I could come up with (short of going into Lifton's rules of totalist elements) was simply I was one of the trees in the forest. When I became a believer in Jesus there was no organized fellowship and as the group developed I moved along with it for all the good and bad it accomplished. I didn't notice a change in my personality. But my friends (Barry, Kenny B. and Ken W.) certainly did. They pointed out to me how I was not the open and caring person they knew but became closed, stern and a bit depressed. I told them, "Gee, thanks guys, why didn't you tell me earlier and save my parents tens of thousands of dollars". They knew then my sense of humor returned and we could all relax.

Coincidentally, my ten year high school reunion was held later in August which Geri and I attended at the Roostertail restaurant and conference hall where my high school prom occurred. The city of Detroit hosts speed boat races on the Detroit River and the name

"Roostertail" refers to the spray created by a fast-moving boat. It was a fun evening and I hadn't received so much attention in a long time. It was like I was a celebrity. Of course, bringing the prettiest lady didn't hurt.

By mid-September, we rented a home in Oak Park, Michigan about two blocks from my first home as a child. It was now a multi-cultural neighborhood with African-Americans, Chaldeans and many orthodox Jews; very different from the white, Mormon area in Spokane we just moved from. It was a great place for a new start. No one knew our background and unless someone became a close friend, Geri and I decided to withhold the negative information regarding the fellowship. Our children played with neighborhood kids, Geri made new friends and I worked. We were becoming an "American Family". Sometimes it was hard to shake off the feeling of having missed out on the good things in life, but what are we to do? We moved on.

It was time to start looking for a church to attend. We felt it important to gather with others of similar faith and for our children to have grounding in God outside of family devotionals. I wanted to attend a church that wouldn't judge us for our mistakes, had sound bible teaching and music we could enjoy.

We decided to start with some main stream protestant churches. Methodists, Lutherans, Baptists; we visited them all. Personally, I wasn't interested in the Catholic Church. Although there are won-derful Christians in attendance, the liturgy is too much for me to handle. After visiting five or six churches over a month's time and asking questions of attendees and pastors, it dawned on us who the best people are to talk to about a specific church. If one wants to get the real scoop on where a church stands on doctrines and issues, talk to the church secretary. This saves time in two areas: visiting tons of churches on Sundays and getting the inside story of where an individual church stands on denominational issues. For example, a denomination may believe a person needs to be water baptized by their church but the local church of that denomination may have a differing view (such as a baptism anywhere will suffice).

While I was at work during the week, Geri would make calls and grill the secretaries on the many questions we had. We narrowed our list of churches to visit to six or seven, based on doctrines, local practices, and location. We really enjoyed our visits with Highland Park Baptist Church in Southfield, Michigan. The people were kind, the teaching from the pulpit strong and the music inspired us. There was also a nursery and Sunday school for the kids which were a novelty for us. David, one of my high school football coaches, is a Christian and when I told him about our search he told me his dad was the architect for the building; what a small world.

We decided to visit one more church (our fifteenth), Brotherhood Christian Church in Royal Oak. It was small, about 125 people, and the services were high-energy with a band that used contemporary music for worship. The sermons by the pastors were very good and seemed meant just for me. The messages gave me comfort and confidence in the Lord. We attended on Sundays and Wednesdays for three weeks and decided BCC is our home church. The love and encouragement of God seemed to ooze out of every member toward my family.

The pastors preached the gospel of Jesus Christ, gave an alter call for prayer every Sunday and held water baptisms frequently. The church believes in the infilling of the Holy Spirit whereby all people can have the love and power of Jesus in their lives on a daily basis. Each person having a personal relationship with Jesus was tantamount to all other doctrines and issues. Brotherhood was an independent church which probably has doctrines most closely aligned with the Assemblies of God denomination. There was one major difference; Brotherhood believes in the "oneness" of God doctrine. Simply stated, there is one God with many manifestations, not a Trinity (God in three persons). That teaching goes beyond the scope of this writing but suffice it to say, it is not a salvation issue to me and being a Jewish Christian, I could live with their interpretation of who God is. I do not feel shaken in my beliefs because I don't see eye to eye with someone. Of course, the people in BCC had nothing but the love and grace of God and did not allow other interpretations of the Godhead to get in the way of relationships. This revelation of having doctrinal differences is very important regarding our recovery.

I started to feel comfortable, but not entirely settled. I had a job, a roof over my family and food on the table. We had a church family

I could count on in a pinch and we had family devotions on a consistent basis. Something was missing and I couldn't put my finger on it. There were some lingering doubts as to falling prey to another type of bible cult. Geri and I talked about it and came to the conclusion that the problem with the fellowship wasn't the doctrines and living for the Messiah, but rather, the practice of leadership, authority, and living under the law of men versus the love and grace of God. We now had the tools to recognize problems in leadership. No more doubts.

I recall a time in the early fall when my parents came over for dinner and they asked us how we became Christians. It was gratifying to tell our story to my parents without the hell, fire and brimstone as I had done in the past. It was a wonderful evening and the love of God filled the house.

Geri and I decided to observe Christmas in a more traditional manner. We bought a tree, ornaments and lights to hang. I never did this before and it really adds beauty to a home. I began to appreciate the joy of the season of recognizing the birth of the Lord our Savior. The Christmas Sunday sermon at BCC was very good. In fact, it seemed to me, the whole service had God's Holy Spirit directing it. Traditional Christmas music was played. There was prayer for healing people who were sick and then the senior pastor, Hal Ballew, got up and gave a message on why the world needs Jesus. I shed tears and remembered why I became a follower of the Messiah. He is fully God and fully man. We are sinners in need of forgiveness and a way for eternal life. Jesus gave His all and did it all! He is the Eternal Light and shared our griefs and sorrows. This particular morning, I felt engulfed by the heavens and His all encompassing Love. In spite of all my mistakes and problems, Jesus loves me. He died and rose from the dead for me. He is the Truth, the Way and the Life. I had no more doubts, no more feelings of being unsettled. I felt born again, again!

A friend of mine told me a few months ago what he thought of my breakthrough. He believes I had all the *facts* from my original search for the Messiah during my college days and discovered my *faith* in God to make it through the interventions and deprogrammings. During Christmas of 1983, I experienced the *feelings* to have a complete relationship with Jesus. It is hard to argue with that theory.

Although my re-integration into society continued for a year or two, the basics were in place. In the spring 1984, Geri read an article about David Wilkerson and his family. David was a preacher who wrote a best selling book ("The Cross and the Switchblade") and started a couple para-churches called Teen Challenge and World Challenge. Until his death in the spring of 2011 he was the senior pastor at Times Square Church in New York City. I knew David had a visit from Doug Keller a few years earlier. David's son, Gary, was a pastor at "Church in the City" located on Woodward Avenue in downtown Detroit. Geri and I began attending Wednesday Services there and we were excited about being part of a ministry to poor people and drug addicts. It was much different than the suburbs.

Soon, we heard that David would be in Detroit and I asked Gary if he would arrange an appointment. David was very gracious with his time and we discussed the fellowship and the leadership. He told us the story of how Doug Keller visited him in Texas and said that he (David) should repent and change the direction of his ministry. David said it was an odd meeting and dismissed it out of hand. He told us we were on the right path and simply keep our eyes and hearts following God. It was simple advice, yet powerful.

I wrote Doug a letter to let him know my reasons for leaving the group, expressing my hope to see him sometime and wishing my best for his family. Doug wrote back with good wishes for me and my family and perhaps reconciliation between us would come available at some future date.

At the beginning of summer 1984, Sheldon, formerly of Ben Israel Ministries and now pastor of a Phoenix, Arizona Jewish messianic congregation, contacted me and said he was travelling to Urbana to visit Doug (who by this time moved back to Illinois). Sheldon asked me to join him at the Sunday service in July. Geri and I were planning a summer visit to see her family in Urbana and decided that would be a good weekend to go.

The meeting began plain enough. We were welcomed and everyone was friendly. Music worship was good. Someone accompanied on guitar. However, there was a turn for the worse. Susan

Katzman, a close friend and one of Geri's bridal attendants, came forward, placed her hand on Geri's shoulder and started to prophesy. Susan said Geri, due to her disobedience, would die the same death as her mother (cancer). The implication was clear. People were upset Geri and I left the group and wanted to let us know. Of course, they felt the need to invoke God's name in place of their own insecurities. Geri was very cool about it. She simply said to everyone that the message was wrong and not from God. Soon thereafter, Eddie Everett, one of the elders, said God was displeased with me and I had a mocking spirit. I knew immediately why he said it. Geri was across the room holding our youngest child during worship time and I was gesturing my pleasure on how much I enjoyed the music. Ed mistook my actions as disrespectful.

Finally, Doug got up and spoke. He eventually got around to me in his speech and told me in front of everyone that due to my disobedience my marriage bed would be defiled. I did not like being called out in front of others, but I dismissed his thought as irrational and erroneous. I could see so clearly their antics and knew all this was not from God but from their own frustrations. I believe God would never use a personal prophecy to embarrass a person in front of others. There is no scriptural basis for it. If someone speaks for, or in the name of God, it had better be from scripture and with compassion. Shelly stood up and gave a brief sermon on how God cleans out his house. Shelly told me later it was a message for the fellowship to get on the right path.

This string of events gave me a solidifying confirmation that our decision to leave the fellowship was right. The meeting gave us a glimpse into the reality of the fellowship and we are so glad we left the group. Sure, we miss our close friends in Urbana and Spokane, but it is a higher and more important thing to do what is right for my family and me.

A couple weeks later Geri and I went out to dinner with my parents. We told them of our trip to Urbana and our visit to a fellowship meeting. They were very upset that we would even consider going. We told them it brought closure to the situation, we held firm while in Urbana and to please trust us. We informed mom how important her intervention meant to us. I explained to her that as a mother, not only did she give me life at birth but through most recent events, she literally saved my life from a destructive lifestyle. We sensed a peace in her heart that we were fully released from the authority which enslaved us. Then Geri and I thanked mom and dad for all they did to help us leave the fellowship. We had a wonderful cry together.

AFTERWORD

Here we are, at the time of this writing, several years after our interventions, deprogrammings and re-integration into society. Our three children are grown and have moved onto productive lives of their own. They seemed to be unscathed by behaviors caused by the fellowship mentality and all three have a faith in God. I received a job offer so Geri and I moved back to Champaign County, Illinois in 1985 and have been attending a church moved by the Spirit of God and led by Godly men and women who have the utmost integrity. I am involved in several ministries at the church. There are few things more fulfilling for me than to do the work of God.

We witnessed some terrible and amazing things pertaining to the fellowship. There are so many details of what transpired from 1983 to 1988 that an entire volume could be written. I will leave that task to others, but a couple of events involving the fellowship drew the attention of society and its legal system.

In 1983, I was the last to be abducted from the group and many others saw the light and left the group on their own accord. The leadership huddled and decided to capture other churches into their fold. The plan usually failed and when it did the leaders took umbrage.

In February 1986, Doug Keller and three other men from the fellowship were convicted in a Champaign County court on felony charges of mob action and misdemeanor charges of criminal damage to property after disrupting a youth service at a church in Urbana in November 1985. The men shouted at the people attending the service and made proclamations against the church and its pastors. They threw a cake containing garbage and chicken bones on the alter.

Keller and the others were sentenced to 11 days in jail and probation. Doug had the strictest probation rules. He could not leave the county without the judge's permission. Before his sentence, Keller said he did not intend any violence and that he was only trying to proclaim God's warning. "I have no right to physically force people to make that choice, but I have the right to proclaim," he said in court. The judge, who is Jewish, said the incident had "overtones of religious bigotry." He also said in court, "There are overtones of people who have taken upon themselves the claim that they are acting in the word of God to the extent that others are to be disregarded. That strikes a nerve."

The fellowship as a whole felt that they, like the first century Christians, were being persecuted for their faith; for the sake of righteousness. They believe they were prosecuted because the Gospel was not obeyed by the men they sought to come under their authority.

Legalism within the group escalated. They became even more closed off from society, shunning people who left the group or wouldn't even discuss the Gospel. Members would not speak with their families for long periods of time. The doctrine of authority (totalism) grew after I left the group. People would stand up and confess their sins in front of the group. Grown men and women were given a spanking – some in a public meeting - for their sin and disobediences. To their credit, there were no sexual encounters that other notorious groups encountered. Nevertheless, the group was in a vicious cycle destroying peoples' lives.

In December, 1987 Keller was granted a release from his probation and immediately jetted off to Spokane, Washington to visit the group. By December 20th, a 14 year old boy was dead. Despite warnings by the women in the fellowship, he was left untreated for child onset diabetes. The boy had also been spanked the day before he died. The pain, as Doug Keller explained it, the boy was going through was blamed on the boy's sin.

In an interview, Keller said the members of the fellowship distrusted doctors and believed in prayer for healing, but said they do not deny anyone medical care. He said members of the fellowship believe sickness is caused by sin and a wicked lifestyle; the best way to get rid of the illness is to get rid of the sin.

Obviously, this was a sad, sad day in the annals of the fellowship.

In very short order, the elders in the various satellite groups of the fellowship received the wake up call. Within 30 days, the groups in New Jersey, Texas and Spokane disbanded. By April, the flagship Urbana group folded. From a very bad event of a young boy's death, very good things happened. Over 300 people from across the country were set free from the stranglehold of their church leadership.

Many people were reunited with their parents. Families were released from the shackles of authority and were free to worship God as they believed. Understandably, many did not know what to believe or where to turn. They were paralyzed from a lack of inter-action with society as a whole. Some couples divorced and some people turned away from Jesus. Many based their beliefs on what they were taught and those teachings were gone along with the cred-ibility of those who taught. Some were very angry at the way the groups broke up. There was no instruction by the fellowship leaders what to do next.

Dozens of former members poured into churches around Champaign-Urbana. We were happy to receive them. Friendships with close friends were restored. Geri's oldest, dearest friend Debra, who had written a letter four years earlier, saying she couldn't visit us, was now embracing us. We were very happy to reunite with her for friendship that lasts to today.

Over the next several months, virtually every elder and leader of the various geographic groups sought out people they wronged. To those who would listen, these men would apologize for any and all wrong doings they did. It was gratifying to me to see these men own up to the hardship they caused. They repented to God and apologized to each person that would allow it. The grace of God was like a cup running over. Although many people were and still are emotionally hurt and scarred, many leaders of the fellowship did their best to make things right.

Geri and I sat in Doug Keller's living room for one of these sessions. His wife, Susan, was there. I could tell Doug had been crying for days and was distraught over the death of the Spokane boy. Doug told us he has been repenting to God and asking forgiveness. He recalled he said some very negative things to us after we left the group and in a very emotional manner asked for our forgiveness. Geri and I immediately accepted Doug's apology. Although he has no spiritual credibility as a leader to me I can certainly love him with the love of God and forgive him for personal wrongdoings.

I also had a session with Eddie Everett which turned out to be a little more lighthearted. After espousing his theory why the fellowship went wrong, Eddie apologized for his behavior at the fellowship meeting in the summer of 1984 for calling me a mocker of the saints. I was surprised he remembered the incident. We ended up laughing when I told him Geri and I were actually making faces to each other in appreciation of and not mocking the fellowship. Eddie and I have been friends since.

Ed Schwan and I had a sit down as well. Ed was an elder and probably my closest friend in the group. He never did me or my family harm. Yet, I am so glad he came to me to patch up our relationship. He had several issues to clear up with members of the group and I told him I was there to support him. Shortly thereafter, I hired Ed in the insurance business and he is now a thriving professional in the St. Louis area.

Doug and another Spokane elder, Jeff Silverman, along with the dead boy's father were convicted of second degree criminal mistreatment, a Class C felony. After the trial and before sentencing, Doug asked the Pastor of our church in Champaign if he could attend on Sundays. The pastor had a meeting with all the former fellowship members (both older and newer) and asked if it was OK for Doug to attend. It was a unanimous "YES," which surprised the pastor. Doug was a broken man who saw the massive errors of his ways. We knew he needed to attend church somewhere and why not a place where people knew him best and keep an eye on him.

Eventually, Doug served two years in prison and came home to Urbana. He has a small business that helps high school and college students perform better as athletes. This is an area that Doug has expertise. He lives a quiet life; raised three wonderful children and I have the highest regard for his wife.

My high school athletic department started a golf outing fundraiser in 1990. Former athletes from the school's inception (1968) to the present attend each year. It was fun to hear how our athletic exploits became more exaggerated over the years. It couldn't get too out of hand as the coaches also attended the golf outing and kept our stories in line with the truth. I also re-established my relationship with the University of Illinois football program. Although I was not a starter in my college years I nevertheless had an important role on the team. I take pride in my (long-gone) abilities to help the team prepare for our opponents. Coaches, lettermen and participants gather each spring for a reunion and during special home games in the fall.

After I left the fellowship, there has been great improvement in my relationship with my mom and the rest of the family. Mom celebrated her 80th birthday and as a gift my brother purchased studio time to record a CD. She still has a great voice and I will treasure the music for a long time. My lack of communication during the fellowship years has now turned into a steady stream of visits for family reunions, Florida vacations and emails.

Of course, having grand children is always a benefit to bring healing in a family. Throughout the years, I drove my family 400 miles to the Detroit suburbs for our annual family reunion. During a long weekend, we'd stay at a hotel, perhaps catch a game at Tiger Stadium (now Comerica Park), have a Bar-B-Que at my sister's house and a cousins' club meeting (more like a "swim-fest") at a local country club. It was great fun becoming reacquainted with my aunts, uncles, cousins and friends.

I recall leaving the fellowship group when I was thirty years old but felt eighteen. While in the group we were caught up in such a cocoon I didn't experience things in the world as others would. After, I became better equipped to handle the joys and pitfalls of life. Birthdays, anniversaries, and the politics of work and life became more meaningful to me. I went through two kidnappings for two different purposes. The first was to restrain me from a faith that was not considered normal for a Jew; the second intervention was to rescue my mind from a destructive cult. I thank God for helping me through both experiences.

I went through a lot of travail in the group but never felt over-burdened. The redemptive work of Jesus is tantamount on my mind and in my heart. It is difficult for me to turn my back on the gospel. He did all the work for life eternal, as the old song goes;

"He paid a debt He did not owe; I owed a debt I could not pay;
I needed someone to wash my sins away.
And, now, I sing a brand new song, "Amazing Grace."
Christ Jesus paid a debt that I could never pay". (written by Ellis J. Crum)

The God of Abraham made a way for Jews and Gentiles to have a personal relationship with Him. I look forward to the future and regardless of what may unfold in life, God is always with me.

CPSIA information can be obtained at www.ICGtesting.com
Printed in the USA
LVOW041938221211

260762LV00003B/1/P

9 781619 040533